I REMEMBER JULIA

I REMEMBER JULIA

Voices of the Disappeared

Eric Stener Carlson

TEMPLE UNIVERSITY PRESS   Philadelphia

Temple University Press, Philadelphia 19122
© 1996 by Eric Stener Carlson
All rights reserved
Published 1996
Printed in the United States of America

Library of Congress Cataloguing-in-Publication Data

Carlson, Eric Stener.
    I remember Julia : voices of the disappeared / Eric
Stener Carlson.
        p.   cm.
    Includes index.
    ISBN 1-56639-430-9 (alk. paper). —
    ISBN 1-56639-437-6 (pbk. : alk. paper)
    1. Disappeared persons—Argentina.
    2. Human rights—Argentina. I. Title.
HV6322.3.A7C37   1996
323.4'9'0992—dc20   96–5021

*Epigraph copyright 1948 by Stuart Gilbert, copyright 1947 by Librairie Galli-
mard. Originally published in France as* La Peste *by Librairie Gallimard and
in the United States by Alfred A. Knopf, Inc., in 1948, pp. 36–37.*

He tried to recall what he had read about the disease. Figures floated across his memory, and he recalled that some thirty or so great plagues known to history had accounted for nearly a hundred million deaths. But what are a hundred million deaths? When one has served in a war, one hardly knows what a dead man is, after a while. And since a dead man has no substance unless one has actually seen him dead, a hundred million corpses broadcast through history are no more than a puff of smoke in the imagination. . . . Ten thousand dead made about five times the audience in a biggish cinema. Yes, that was how it should be done. You should collect the people at the exits of five picture-houses, you should lead them to a city square and make them die in heaps if you wanted to get a clear notion of what it means. Then at least you could add some familiar faces to the anonymous mass. But naturally that was impossible to put into practice; moreover, what man knows ten thousand faces?
—from Albert Camus, *The Plague*

CONTENTS

ACKNOWLEDGMENTS

Although this is Julia's story, I cannot, in all conscience, dedicate this work to her. The truth cannot benefit the dead, only the living. And if what follows comes close to being the truth of who Julia was, of what she did and said, then I dedicate this work to the living, those who knew her, those who talk. I give my thanks to all those people who contributed their time and insights so that this story could be told. Although it is impossible to mention everyone, I would like to especially thank the Equipo Argentino de Antropología Forense; the Centro de Estudios Legales y Sociales; and the Fulbright Commission, whose grant made this investigation possible. Thanks also to every Argentine who opened his or her home, heart, and family to me, who trusted a stranger enough to share that which is most precious—their memories of Julia.

The characters and events described in this book are historically accurate, as are the names of the torture centers in Buenos Aires in which Julia was held. The names of certain individuals, however, and the locations and dates of certain events have been modified in order to protect the privacy of those persons who otherwise would not have been willing to add to this account. It is a testimony to the pain and fear still surrounding the disappearance of the woman whose story appears in the following pages that, almost twenty years after her death, the reader cannot know her real name. The author finds it ironic that he is compelled to take "Julia's" real name away from her in order to promote her memory, for it is the name, first of all, that this disappeared person was robbed of when she was kidnapped. Her name, and thus her identity, her liberty, and her life.

AUTHOR'S INTRODUCTION

In June of 1991, I traveled to Argentina as a volunteer for the Equipo Argentino de Antropología Forense, or Argentine Forensic Anthropology Team. I spent two months working with this team of archaeologists and doctors in a site already under excavation in the cemetery of Avellaneda, a city on the outskirts of Buenos Aires. There, among the imposing tombs and mausoleums of some of Argentina's less well known statesmen and military heroes, we divided off an abandoned section of land into grids and slowly began to shave down the earth centimeter by centimeter with sharpened trowels. As the bones began to appear, we dusted them off with small brushes, recording their positions in the ground.

Avellaneda was the site of a mass grave of "disappeared" people, or *desaparecidos*, murder victims of Argentina's most recent military dictatorship, the *Proceso de Reorganización Nacional* (Process of National Reorganization, 1976–1982). By the time the excavation was completed, the team had uncovered the skeletons of close to four hundred people—men, women, and children—many with obvious signs of having been executed by nine-millimeter pistol and machine gun rounds.

Avellaneda is but one example of the mass graves spread throughout Argentina, a depository for the Armed Forces' campaign of kidnapping and mass murder, or "Dirty War," allegedly for the purpose of eradicating urban terrorism. The National Commission on the Disappearance of People (CONADEP), created by the democratic government of President Raúl Alfonsin in 1983 to investigate human rights violations, initially set the number of disappeared at 8,960. Later, official estimates ranged to ten thousand, while national and international human rights organizations independent of the government have set the figure as high as thirty thousand.

One day in July, as I sat in the graveyard, washing the soil off one set of bones I had recently uncovered and letting them dry in the sun, I began to wonder who this person had been whose bones I was handling. From the pelvis and the configuration of the skull, we could often determine whether the victim was male or female. Height could be established fairly well, and so could age.

But who was this person? What had he or she been like? Who were all of them, body piled on top of body, sometimes thirteen deep in a grave?

CONADEP's final report, entitled *Nunca Más (Never Again)*, describes cases of extrajudicial arrest, detention in at least 340 clandestine prison camps throughout the country, torture—including electrocution with cattle prods, rape, drowning, beatings—and mass murder. Although the Argentine soil has been described in some cases as being virtually saturated with corpses as a result of this process, identification of victims' remains has been possible only in a limited number of cases. Very few X-rays of the kidnap victims, prior to their deaths, have survived the passing of time. Without such documentation, to compare a victim's known bone structure (including distinguishing fractures caused by childhood accidents, dental work, and natural defects) against the remains uncovered by the archaeological team, there is little chance of identification.

When a murder victim is identified (the rare exception rather than the norm), the surviving family members are contacted, and those that wish may gather for a memorial service, often in the same cemetery where the remains were discovered. Some words are said about this person's life, friends and relatives cry, and the cemetery custodian places the small box of bones in the family niche and then locks the door. The families, still crying, the older members leaning on the younger ones, the younger ones not quite sure what it is they've seen, leave the labyrinth of tombs and return home. Here the story ends. The skeleton now has a nameplate; perhaps a photograph is placed beside it. Several such photos can be seen in Avellaneda through the dusty glass of the small crypts: yellowed paper pinned to silver frames.

That day in July, I tried to imagine the bones that I was cataloging with a black felt-tip pen—the grid number where they had been found and the date—as having been part of a person that walked and lived and breathed, and I found it very difficult.

So many times the disappeared seem removed from our reality. We suppose that they were once alive because we can see what is left of them—bones, bits of clothing, photographs—but because we lack a person, a personality, to connect our lives with theirs, we find it extremely hard to imagine that each one, in fact, had been a real person. In this way, ten thousand dead, twenty thousand, thirty thousand come to be mere numbers, arbitrary and lacking in humanity.

Indeed, even in the face of overwhelming evidence collected by the anthropologists, and even after recent admissions from "repentant" soldiers that hundreds of victims of the military regime had been drugged and tossed into the sea to die, there are still many Argentines who maintain that there are no disappeared people, a common piece of conversation overheard in the open air cafés of Buenos Aires and in the long lines outside its cinemas. There are also those who concede that there were "excesses" committed by the Armed Forces, and who justify them as tragic but unavoidable consequences of a war against subversion. In all of this discourse of guilt-shifting and recrimination—which group was more right or more wrong, the military or the revolutionaries—the people who were murdered in this process are nowhere to be found. They are still disappeared in many ways, even after their exhumations have been performed.

As I put the bones in a cardboard box and stood to place them in the nearby morgue for storage, I saw the apartment complexes rising over the low-lying walls of the cemetery, which had been standing long before the military dictatorship. I imagined the people living in those apartments, who saw the military trucks pass by year after year in the night and unload stacks of bodies under the electric lights. They all knew what was going on. They all knew, and yet they never said a word. I thought to myself, What could be said of the disappeared if they wouldn't speak?

I began to think of all the other unknown lives stacked away neatly in the cardboard boxes on the shelves of the morgue. I thought of all the families left behind when their sons or daughters, wives and husbands, were made to disappear. There had to have been people before the disappearances, before there were bones and graves and grieving mothers. There had to be people who would talk. . . .

What appears in the following pages is the result of more than two years of investigation and research into the life of one disappeared person. Out of the many lives worthy of investigation in the cemetery of Avellaneda (indeed, in all of Argentina) I have selected a young woman whom I call Julia Andrea Montesini. The reasons for my selecting Julia are above all practical. In the first place, there was a great deal of forensic evidence available that positively identified her as a murder victim of the Argentine military. Second, she was survived by people able to perform a second exhumation—emotional, psychological—those willing and brave enough to talk about what type of person Julia had been.

Whereas there is a great deal of literature available on the political and economic effects produced by the dictatorship upon Argentine society, thorough analysis of books written about the Dirty War, there has been little attention paid to the voices of the people who lived through those dark times. My intention is to take a new approach, to begin to listen. Therefore, in my presentation I have taken great pains to exclude quotations from secondary sources, focusing instead upon the voices of those persons directly involved. I write down the words of these survivors of the Dirty War from conversations that I tape-recorded, face to face with them, in kitchens, cafés, offices, and living rooms throughout Argentina, from the summer of 1991 to the spring of 1993. What follows here is neither a political treatise nor an anthropological study. Rather, it comprises brief sketches, outlines of the personalities of those who knew Julia, vignettes of who she was, memories of what she meant to them. This style of writing may prove bothersome to those readers accustomed to an extensive bibliography, but, after all, the story of Julia is not something provable, palpable. It is an opinion, and she is an idea that lives in people's minds. I leave it to other authors to paint their pictures from the "scholarly" sources.

It is impossible, however, to present these personal histories without touching upon the larger historical and political events that formed the background of Julia's disappearance. I have also included interviews with Argentine experts in the field of human rights. Here, in their own voices, the soldiers, politicians, activists, and priests tell their own stories of the disappeared.

I am forced to say in this introduction that there are many people who do not want this story to be told, not only the soldiers and policemen responsible for Julia's death but also many of those who knew her as friends. They ask me, "Why bring this up, after all these years, if the only consequence will be to bring back memories of fear and pain?"

In responding to this question, I am reminded of my former college literature teacher, Arnoŝt Lustig, a writer on the Holocaust. He recounted that one day, as he was in the synagogue relating some of his experiences as a prisoner in the concentration camps, he was shouted down by some of the people present, who said, "You shouldn't bring this up, Arnoŝt. It is better to forget all of this ugliness."

Arnoŝt responded with a story. One winter day in 1944, as he was walking about an anonymous prison compound in Auschwitz-Birkenau, he felt terribly cold, drained of energy. As he began to walk more and more slowly, he realized that he was freezing to death, and that he would soon collapse. Suddenly, a group of men who had been wandering on the fringe of the compound gathered around him and pressed their bodies together, raising his temperature through their body heat. They stayed only for a short time, and then they dispersed, and Arnošt never saw them again.

Arnošt said that this is why he talks about the Holocaust, this is why he reminds people what it was like. Although it was ugly, although it was terrible, there was one beautiful moment when people gathered together to save his life, and this act of human solidarity had to be remembered.

That is how I view this presentation of voices, as strangers huddling in the cold, trying to preserve not a life, but the memory of one, a memory of Julia. And it is cold today in Argentina, when it is considered socially and politically best not to touch upon the subject of the disappeared, best to forget and to go on.

But these people do not gather for Julia's sake alone. They also gather for themselves. Julia is the silver cord running through their very different lives. Doctors, secretaries, prisoners—strangers among themselves—they are bound together by her, because the day that Julia disappeared, she did not disappear alone.

Each person who knew Julia disappeared a bit that day— psychologically, emotionally—many denying for years that they ever knew Julia for fear of being made to disappear as well, others changing jobs, quitting schools, because they couldn't stand the memories that such places held for them. Some ran away, and some are still running. Here, the storytellers give pieces of their own lives as they talk, filtering the memories of Julia through their own experiences. Sometimes it is a song. Sometimes it is a poem. Sometimes it appears to be a mad rambling of the miserable and the despised. But it is always Julia, and it is a part of them as well.

To say, "I remember Julia" for them is not only an act of memory but also an act of faith, an act of love. What follows is quite a simple story. There was once a young woman named Julia. She had a family and friends who loved her very much. Then, one day, she was kidnapped by a section of the Argentine Armed Forces, she was held for several months in a series of concentration camps, and then she was murdered.

This is an elegy for the dead, and a chance for the living to reclaim a memory of someone who touched their lives in a very special way, someone whom they cannot forget, someone who is not just another number in an unmarked grave.

I REMEMBER JULIA

1

The Cemetery

It was noon on an early May day, 1991, the sun's rays barely reaching over the long shadow of row upon row of family crypts. The priest stood in the whitewashed chapel. His arms outspread, he spoke a few words to the people gathered there about justice, love, and remembrance. Fourteen years after her death, the ritual of burial for Julia Andrea Montesini had begun.

A man named Manuel began to argue with the priest. He shouted and cried, becoming almost hysterical. What had disturbed him most was the band of policemen keeping watch on the fringe of the ceremony. To him, it was as if the Argentine security services that had murdered Julia were enjoying the last act of the show, gloating in their victory. When asked why they were there, they replied, "to provide order." After all, this was one of the first identifications and reburials of a disappeared person in Avellaneda since the return of the civilian government in 1983. They had expected at least two hundred people to attend, the policemen said. Little more then twenty did.

The crowd was relatively small, but like a scene from a Greek tragedy, everyone donned a mask to represent the larger force that brought them to the cemetery that day. They were all present—the innocent, the dead, the guilty, and the lost.

Representatives from the Mothers of the Plaza de Mayo were there, wearing their distinctive white kerchiefs, embroidered with the names of their children, like Julia, who had been made to disappear forever by the military government. There were doctors from the hospital where Julia had worked, family members, and friends. The Grandmothers of the Plaza de Mayo were also present, women whose daughters or daughters-in-law like Julia had been kidnapped while pregnant, and the fate of their missing grandchildren remained unknown.

A few hundred meters from where the burial ceremony was taking place, the Argentine Forensic Anthropology Team had discovered Julia's remains the year before. She had been buried in a clandestine grave site within the cemetery walls, along with 334 other corpses registered merely as NN, or *nihel nomen* in Latin, the nameless ones.

Patricia "Pato" Bernardi, the president of the Team, remembers working at the graveyard the day Julia's remains were unearthed. Of all the sectors into which the Team had divided the excavation site, Patricia remembers that the going was most difficult in sector 135. Covered by years of garbage tossed over the cemetery wall by neighbors, it was, in an archeological sense, a complete nightmare. Adding to the problems was the wet weather that wreaked havoc with the earth, mixing the various levels of bricks and metal springs—even a bed post, Patricia recalls—with the human remains. But then, as Patricia describes, at a lower level during the month of February 1990, the archaeologists

> began to see the disposition of skeletons in a more coherent form, more articulated. . . . Three skeletons appeared, which we determined were female. We were working . . . and someone says to

me, "Oy, there's something strange inside this one." Well, Alejandro [the Team's medical doctor] was there, and we asked him "Hey, what could have happened so that a person could have this in his sternum?"

What Patricia referred to was a series of surgical wires running through the sternum of a skeleton that would be known from that day on as #17. Alejandro said that he thought it could be the result of a heart operation. Patricia doesn't know why, but as soon as she heard Alejandro's explanation, she felt sure she knew whose remains they had just discovered.

Out of the reams and reams of notes collected by the anthropologists from family members of the disappeared—notebooks filled with physical information, bone defects, medical histories—Patricia says:

> We had divided the information according to the clandestine detention centers. I was in charge of the Pozo de Banfield. There were things that I knew by memory, for example that one of the women who had been seen in the Pozo de Banfield had undergone a heart operation one year before her kidnapping. This point remained recorded inside of me. Because of this, when Alejandro confirmed that they were suture wires, I immediately remembered Julia Andrea Montesini.

When the anthropologists removed the skeleton and took it to the morgue to be washed, they found that the skull had been completely shattered by a gunshot blast, and it was impossible to reconstruct in its entirety. Moreover, there was no way to determine the exact day, month, or even year of the murder. As Patricia relates, the forensic team concluded in its final report:

> Concerning the cause of death of skeleton #17 we can say that the same was produced by the passage of a projectile from a firearm through the cranium, which caused severe damage to the brain. Additionally, fragments of a firearm projectile were recovered during the archeological excavation.

From calculations made from the victim's coccyx, the anthropologists determined that she had been thirty years old at the time of death, plus or minus two years, and they estimated her height at about 157 centimeters plus or minus 3.55 centimeters. Following Patricia's hunch, this fit almost exactly the age and height of Dr. Julia Andrea Montesini, missing since March 1977. Additionally, what is termed a preauricular notch was found on the remains of the pelvis, a mark often caused by the extreme pressure produced during childbirth. (If this, indeed, were Julia, the appearance of the notch would follow, as she had been two months pregnant at the time of her kidnapping.) Finally, the anthropologists took note of the extensive dental reconstruction in the skull of skeleton #17, and Patricia remembers thinking, "What bad teeth for such a young girl."

The surviving brother, Manuel, was asked to come to Avellaneda, and the anthropologists began the difficult task of asking him questions about Julia's physical composition, what she had looked like, trying to match the description of this young woman to the bones they had found. The age, the height, the wires in the sternum, even the preauricular notch seemed to point to a positive identification, and yet it was impossible to state without doubt that skeleton #17 was that of Julia. Literally thousands of women Julia's age and height had been kidnapped by the military; of those, it was impossible to say how many could have been pregnant, or how many possibly could have had heart operations. It was a terrible time of doubt, Patricia remembers. Manuel was so close to finding his only sister after all these years, but he had no way of knowing for sure.

Tired and depressed, Manuel and the anthropologists retired to a small café near the graveyard to talk. As they sat in this nether zone of hope and desperation, the coffee finished, a bottle of wine opened, they drank in silence. Patricia shuffled through the fragments of information that Manuel could provide. It was all the same old information. Graveyard workers moved in and out, kicking the mud from their boots, leaving their shovels at the door. Nothing that the anthropologists could think of seemed to help. There were no other leads.

And then Manuel looked up and said softly that if it would help at all, he remembered that Julia had suffered from dental problems.

Julia's former orthodontist was immediately contacted by Alejandro and told of the possible identification. Remarkably, this doctor had maintained three sets of files all these years: one for her current patients, one for those who had died or permanently moved away, and a third for those who had disappeared without a trace. It was in this final category that Julia's charts were located, and it was discovered that both upper and lower sets of teeth had been extensively reconstructed. Armed with her files, the orthodontist traveled to Avellaneda and positively identified the prostheses found in the skull of skeleton #17 as her handiwork, including the materials she had used in the operation. It was that day, from a common grave, thirteen years after her disappearance, that Julia once again appeared.

VOICE I

Emilio Fermín Mignone

President of the Centro de Estudios Legales y Sociales
(Center for Legal and Social Studies); author of several
books concerning the military, violence, and democracy in
Argentina; provided testimony against the military junta
before the United Nations and the U.S. Congress.

I have had three functions, more or less public ones, always in the field of education. I was director of education for the province of Buenos Aires in 1949 in the constitutional government of the first presidency of Perón. Afterwards, I was at the Organization of American States in Washington. Later on, I was Sub-secretary of Education in the military government of Onganía. And, well, this was the error of my life. I'm not happy about this. That is to say, I shouldn't have accepted the post. It was a moment in which the government of Onganía was liberalizing, it was changing. They were going to call elections, and I thought that it could be a useful collaboration, and I did some interesting things. Of course, there was no comparison with the dictatorship of 1976–1982.

There were no political prisoners, there was no repression, and of course, there were no assassinations, no disappearances. It was a de facto regime, but it wasn't a cruel regime. There was no repression. It was a normal government. There was a justice system, a fairly well respected government. Its first vice was being de facto, not being a constitutional government, and the second was that it was inept. Either way, it was a military government, and I shouldn't have participated. When you're young it's easy to criticize the old men because they commit mistakes. But it's difficult, as the years go by, to do nothing. If you don't do anything, you never make mistakes.

I had the misfortune that my daughter's detention made me immerse myself in all of this. My daughter was taken on May 14, 1976. It happened almost right after the coup. The revolution was March 24. Therefore, I realized what was going on.

When the soldiers came for my daughter, I thought that they had come to look for me because I had been the director of the university, and there were four, five directors who were held in prison. One of them was made to disappear, was murdered. It was five o'clock in the morning when they came, and they said that they were the army. I was saved, and my wife was saved because we were known abroad. When they finally took us prisoner in 1981, fairly late, there was a large movement for our release.

I made myself study the subject of disappearances, and I began to act. My wife and I adopted three decisions that not everyone adopted. One of the first was to inform everyone that my daughter had been kidnapped. I started by sending a memo to all of the neighbors in the building, telling them about it. Second, to maintain that it had been the Armed Forces that had come, an organized operation that had taken my daughter. The military said, "But they're insurgent groups. They're groups that we don't control." But that wasn't true. The military said, "What barbarity. That's horrible! Yes, I understand. Your

daughter. We'll find out. It's got to be one of those armed groups."
(A lie! I said that this was a lie.) I took a firm and energetic stance.
And third, I resolved to work actively to form a solidarity group for
families of the disappeared people.

Then what happened? Because my house is in the center of the city,
and because I'm more or less well known, dozens of people came to
see me and to tell me their stories. "My son's disappeared. They've
taken away my daughter." So I said, send a letter to Amnesty International, to the Red Cross, go to the curia, go to see the bishop, write a
letter to the Organization of American States, write to the United
Nations, and organize people, to form groups. My wife was one of the
first to become a member of the Mothers of the Plaza de Mayo.

Yes, yes, I was afraid. I received threats by telephone. They wrote
things on the wall in the street in front of my house. They cut the
brake line on my car. I tried to stop myself, and I smashed against a
wall. Another time they filled the motor of my car with sand. They
followed me by car at night. Of course I was afraid. I'm not the brave
kind. But I believed—I still believe—that when someone loses a
daughter in these circumstances, it's not bravery that makes him look
for her.

Guerrilla operations had already begun during the last period of the
Onganía government. Very severe laws were ratified. Afterwards,
some of these laws were abolished during the brief constitutional period of Cámpora at the beginning of 1973 and of Perón in 1974. But
already, after the death of Perón, during the de facto government of
María Estela Martínez de Perón (Perón's wife), Dr. Italo Argentino
Luder took charge of the government. Now a very important event
happened that had to do with repression and the law.

This event consisted in the passing of decrees that called on the
Armed Forces to intervene in the repression. Until that point, the
Armed Forces had acted in defense of the national borders, not in internal disputes. For internal disputes there is the police. In this decree
above all others that Luder signed it states that the objective of the
intervention of the armed forces is *el aniquilamiento* (the extermination)

of the guerrilla. The military has always interpreted *el aniquilamiento* as extermination; that is to say, as death, physical disappearance.

When the trial of the Junta was initiated in 1984, the first person called to testify was Luder, and he said that *el aniquilamiento* should have been interpreted in the sense of war used to end or dominate the will of the enemy; so that, in this case, it meant the extermination of the guerrilla movement, not the extermination of the guerrillas themselves. That is to say, as president, he never signed a document that called for the guerrillas to be killed.

The military has always interpreted *el aniquilamiento* as the extermination of the guerrillas, of those whom it called subversives. Then President Videla said "All the people who harbor thoughts against Western Christian civilization are subversive." In that case, you've got to exterminate half of the country.

The curious part about all of this is that with these decrees the Armed Forces legally had, by way of a constitutional government, first, the capacity to intervene in matters of internal security, and second, the authority to destroy the subversion. They really had everything. Curiously, now when the military tries to defend themselves against the accusations of violations of human rights, they say that they were acting constitutionally, that they were acting legally. But the question I ask is, if they had everything and were acting under the constitutional order, why did they destroy the constitutional regime six months later? They exterminated it, because they carried out a coup d'état. According to the proclamation by which they carried out the coup, it was because the constitutional government wasn't capable of ending the subversion. This is absurd. It shows that they are liars and contradictory because if they were defending the constitutional order, why did they carry out a coup?

There was a famous *comunicado (communiqué)* from the head of the Armed Forces, who was Videla, commander in chief in 1975 (after the defeat of the ERP in Monte Chingolo and the defeat of the Montoneros in Formosa in an attack against a regiment) saying that the armed ability of the subversion had been exterminated: it was over. I believe that he was telling the truth. Everything that was done afterwards was to exterminate those that they considered the infrastructure of the subversion, those who weren't guerrillas themselves or combatants. Rather, they were student activists, activists in high school, activists in factories, intellectuals. All of them, according to the military, were responsible for the subversion, and they had to be exterminated in order to change the country, in order to finish with the subversion. This is the military mentality.

My interpretation is that, first, it's certain that the Armed Forces intervened under orders of the constitutional government. It's certain that their objective was *el aniquilamiento*. But, according to the interpretation of the president of the Republic who signed this decree, *el aniquilamiento* did not mean murder; rather, it meant putting an end to the combative capacity of the enemy, the subversion and not the subversives. The Armed Forces, however, killed the vast majority of their prisoners. And they weren't prisoners taken in combat. They were prisoners taken in their houses. Furthermore, there was a great quantity of people who had nothing to do with the subversion. They weren't combatants; they never held a weapon in their hands. I calculate that no more than five percent of the disappeared people could be called combatants. The number of combatants could not have been more than four hundred, five hundred at the time of the military coup—no more. The great majority were sympathizers; they sympathized more or less with the subversive movements or wanted a revolutionary change.

The military acted with cowardice. That is to say, they used a system, they made themselves into subversives, into guerrillas. They used illegal methods in making people disappear. The death sentence existed, but they never used it. It existed in the civil code. Of course, it existed in the military code. They never applied it because they didn't have the honor or the valor to sign a death sentence.

In an extreme case, the death sentence could have been legal. In order to do this, they could have decreed what is called martial law here. Martial law is established by the constitution. And it establishes that in the country or territory or zone in which martial law is applied, the inhabitants of this zone are subjected to military laws. The military laws permit the establishment of military judges who act in a summary manner. "In a summary manner" means—I'm not saying five minutes—but at least an hour, or half an hour, a summary judgment, that is to say, where the accused is present, someone accuses him, someone defends him, and the judge passes sentence.

This could have been done legally. I'm not saying that it would have been politically or morally acceptable, but it would have been more moral, more morally acceptable than denying that they had the prisoners, torturing them, and killing them, as they did with thirty thousand people. Under martial law, then they at least would have done it openly, but they didn't want to do it, because they knew that this would provoke an international reaction. There was a phrase continually repeated at this time, repeated to me many times by generals and admirals whom I saw in the search for my child: "We are not going to commit the same mistake as Franco or as Pinochet of shooting people publicly in the street, because the Pope himself is going to ask us not to shoot them."

In their cowardice and their ineptitude they wanted to develop a system. General Camps said that the Argentines had discovered the correct method for putting an end to the subversion that other countries were never able to, because they didn't use these methods; above all, Italy and the matter of the Red Brigades. The Argentine method had precedents; they said they had received training from the North American school in Panama, but above all, they said that they had received training from the French insurgency in Indochina and Algeria. (Because the mentality of the French is always closer to the Argentine mentality, because it's Latin.)

Well, they thought, the North Americans lack ideas. They are pragmatists, they can teach these methods of torture, but they don't know why they are doing it. On the other hand, the French, the French paratroopers, always used to talk about God and Western civilization, and our military said the same. But they say we have perfected these methods. The idea was to do this secretly. The Economic Minister Martínez de Hoz explained in an interview that they had to carry out these methods secretly because they didn't want to face the reaction of the developed countries, the opinion of the United States, France, Italy, Spain, countries from which Argentina wanted to ask for help for its economic restoration; above all, because the Carter administration was openly against violations of human rights. Therefore, they believed, in their stupidity and insanity, that this could be done secretly and that no one would realize it.

I am completely convinced that they thought they had discovered the ideal method, because in a way, they were right. For many months the Argentine people were misinformed. All they knew was some neighbor, some relative, a friend, had disappeared, but they didn't know that it was a system. Many Argentines found out the truth after the arrival of democracy. Others claimed that they found out afterwards, but they are hypocritical, and they say "I didn't know anything." It's like Germany during the Nazi era when the Germans always insisted that they didn't know that the concentration camps existed, of the extermination of the Jews. In part, it's true. In part, it's not. I spoke with dozens of military officials during this time, generals, and the answer was "Oh, I'm sorry! What a tragedy! Where could your daughter be? Could she be living in exile, could she be in Paris? Could she be in hiding, or could she be with the guerrillas? Could she have been taken by the guerrillas?" And I said, "Look, let's throw all our cards on the table. I know that whether you tell me or not—you don't want to tell me, you don't want to say that she's here—you're lying to me."

This secret activity was, above all, the work of the intelligence services. Here, in Argentina, there was an excess, an overabundance of intelligence services. The intelligence services were the ones that conceived the system. The intelligence services, all of them, all of the military, have a very partial view of reality. They believed that they could invent this plan and make it work. The State approved of it, and it was applied. They created the so-called *fuerzas de tarea* groups that worked with a great quantity of officials and subofficials. I am convinced that Videla did not point out who was to be killed. There's no doubt about that. But what did he do? He authorized them to capture and to kill these people. He didn't intervene. That's clear. He didn't need to intervene because he had already given the authorization to torture and to kill. He is responsible. That is to say, the leader has to assume responsibility for the decisions that are of such importance as taking a person's life. It can't be left in the hands of a captain, of a colonel, but rather in the hands of the supreme authority.

More than arrogance, it was stupidity. There was arrogance as well, to believe that they were the owners of other people's destinies, that they could manipulate the entire society, fool the entire world. One of the aspirations of my life, what is left of my life, is to see the Armed Forces recognize that their situation was illegitimate and to see that they do so publicly. Without this, there is not going to be reconciliation. We're always going to think that everyone in the military is a torturer and a murderer, even though he's not.

A short while ago, a friend of mine told me about a colonel, a friend of his, who was extremely angry because his thirteen-year-old son had gone to school, and upon finding out that his father was a soldier, his schoolmates asked him, "Did your father used to torture people?" And the colonel said, "This is an affront to the army, that this story has got around." Well, that's going to be how it is as long as the military doesn't say, "We condemn the torturers and we condemn the action of those who hid them." I know that the current head of the Armed Forces is not a torturer, and I know that he wants these things to be forgotten. He says that you've got to forget them, but for this to happen, the military, as an institution, has got to take the step of recognizing the error that they committed and ask forgiveness from the society for having committed these crimes, as an institution.

Videla's great preoccupation was to give an appearance of voting, of Christianity; in reality he was the most hypocritical of all because of this. The others were more ready to do things more openly. But those who pretended to be more gentle, less cruel, at the bottom of it all they were the worst because they were the most hypocritical. If they had shot twenty thousand people in Argentina it would have been an international scandal. They were right in this. Well, they made twenty thousand, thirty thousand people disappear without an international scandal, but in the end the scandal occurred. It came late. In this sense, they won. But in the end, they lost.

11

Catalina

Julia Andrea was always very spoiled. She was the youngest, the one who got the most gifts. She was always a happy child, devoted to her grandparents.

This is how Catalina Garcia de Montesini describes her only daughter, Julia. Almost twenty years now after Julia's death, Catalina says that it's very difficult for her to give a good idea of the kind of person Julia was. She has pockets of memories, pictures of Julia in certain phases, as a small child, as a grown-up. But there is no steady line of memory. There are no anecdotes, no childhood stories. Julia just seems to be in the background of what Catalina says, the feeling of a presence, really, more than a personality. She is an ache difficult to define.

Now eighty-seven years old, Catalina's most instinctive memories are those that have to do with the beginning, when she had just married, when her family was young and starting out. Catalina was born in the small town of La Fuente in the province of Córdoba about twenty hours by bus from the capital of Buenos Aires. It was there that she met her future husband, Eduardo Hector Montesini, also a native of La Fuente. She was a second-generation Argentine, granddaughter of Italian, Basque and Spanish immigrants, the typical European mixture that formed the new wave of Argentines at the turn of the century. He was from the first generation, his parents having recently immigrated from Italy. According to Catalina, theirs had not been a complicated courtship. "We went out as boyfriend and girlfriend," she says. "And then, afterwards, we married." She still remembers the wedding day quite clearly—August 19, 1939.

Eduardo ran the family hotel in La Fuente, saving his money for when he and his wife would move away and begin a life on their own. As Catalina relates,

> About two years after we were married, we moved to Pilar de la Sierra in the same province. My husband bought a hotel there. Pilar is pretty much a small town. The town really lived off the countryside because the farms came together around Pilar. And the people came to town for entertainment and to shop.

Eduardo's place of work was the Hotel de la Sierra, larger than the one his family had owned in La Fuente, quite large, Catalina says with a smile, "with a lobby and two floors." It was there that the Montesinis first lived, before they bought a house of their own in town a few years later.

Cars were still a novelty when Catalina first lived in Pilar de la Sierra. Trucks, however, were an increasing necessity for the *campesinos* (farmers) living on nearby dairy farms. If they needed to drive into town on the rut-filled roads after a heavy rain, it was most probably done by truck. Horse and buggy, however, was still the normal mode of transportation, and Catalina remembers the two horse-drawn services for the inhabitants of the village, delivering fresh bread and milk daily. There was also a clinic nearby, but no ambulance. The

volunteer fire department did, however, maintain an old prop plane
to transport patients to a city hospital in case of emergency.
La Fuente is about sixty kilometers away from Pilar de la Sierra.
Catalina knows the way back and forth quite well. As she explains,
"All three of my children were born in La Fuente because, when they
were about to be born, I went to my mother's house in La Fuente.
And I returned home with the kids each time one of them was born."
Manuel was the oldest, born October 31, 1942. Luis Ignacio was
born on November 6, 1945, and one year later came the last of the
children, Julia Andrea, born on November 21, 1946.

The Montesinis got by in Pilar de la Sierra. They weren't rich,
Catalina insists, but they were not poor either. The economy in Pilar
even began to flourish during the late 1940s, as the surrounding farms
benefited from the grain shortage in war-torn Europe in selling their
crops abroad.

Catalina remembers Julia doing homework in the hotel lobby when
the guests were not around. And there was an old piano in the lobby
on which Julia, always fond of music, would practice. She invited
friends to come and listen to her private debuts. "She was always surrounded by friends," Catalina says, "always sure of herself." She spent
hours practicing in front of the old piano, the worn hammers slowly
striking the chords, the little girl struggling at the pedals.

Catalina's memory jumps from Julia doing her schoolwork in the
hotel lobby to Julia as a young medical student, studying in Córdoba,
the capital of the province of Córdoba. She can't really say why Julia
studied medicine. The Montesinis didn't have any doctors in the family. But Julia was very enthusiastic about her studies, Catalina recalls,
always talking about the work that she was doing. Catalina says, "She
used to study, at least the last two years of medical school she studied
a lot."

Catalina says it's possible that Julia's problems began when she went
away to study in Córdoba. Being the capital of such a large province
and also the home of the university, problems seemed to be magnified
in Cordóba. It was more political, more active. It's possible, Catalina
says softly, that if Julia had stayed away from Córdoba with its danger-

ous politics and ideas, she might still be alive today. But then Catalina admits, "she probably would have disappeared in Pilar de la Sierra, too." She does not doubt the military's capacity to reach in and shatter even the peace of Pilar life, not after the bloody trauma that she and her family lived through more than twenty years earlier, which was known as *la Revolución Libertadora*.

In September 1955, the questionably democratic government of Juan Domingo Perón was threatened by military revolt. Two opposing army factions, one setting out from the nearby army installation of Matamoros and advancing toward Buenos Aires and the other moving from Buenos Aires toward Matamoros, met and clashed one night just outside of Pilar de la Sierra. There were fire fights by the river, Catalina says, and she remembers the bodies found floating there the next day. She also remembers her husband getting out his pistol that night and running toward the door. "He had to go, I don't know where," Catalina says. "He had to deliver a message. He had to take something to someone." Catalina pleaded with him not to leave. She didn't know what was going on, if the government had fallen, why there were army trucks rolling down the streets of Pilar. "In the end," she explains with a sigh, "he didn't go. His friends wouldn't let him go. Some others went instead of him."

As the sound of distant gunfire died down, the soldiers from one of the factions (Catalina doesn't remember which one) took control of the village. The Montesinis, as well as every other family in Pilar, were forced to receive an army conscript into their house, feed him, and give him a place to sleep. She remembers that their soldier was very hungry and cleaned his plate of everything offered to him. "Poor boy," she says. She goes on to say:

> We had a fright that night. There were soldiers all over the place. I had some uncles who lived in Pilar, who lived very close to the plaza. It just so happens that the municipal building, including the police station, is in the plaza. And there, in the plaza, several mortars had been set up. And it just so happens that my uncles were going to sleep in our house that night, because the cannons

were so close to their house. The soldiers made us turn off all the lights. This night, it was all dark outside, and I was afraid that my uncles wouldn't see the house well enough to find their way. They still hadn't come when the soldiers made us turn off all the lights. There wasn't one light in the street. So, every once in a while, I looked out the window to see if I could make out anything, and I saw a big truck filled with weapons. It was there the whole night.

From that dark night in 1955, Catalina's memory skips ahead more than twenty years to another street, another city, and another military takeover.

· Catalina vividly remembers walking down the streets of Córdoba with Julia. It was the day before her daughter was to be married to a young doctor named Alberto Espinoza—May 17, 1976—and Julia had recently graduated from medical school. And yet everything that Catalina saw around her seemed to say that the *Revolución Libertadora* was still in progress, and she remembers wanting so much to protect her little girl. Men in uniforms checked documentation on the street corners. Green Ford Falcons bearing no license plates—the car of choice for the military intelligence services—slowly patrolled the streets, and trucks passed by, picking up people and taking them away.

In the years that had gone by since Pilar de la Sierra was occupied, Catalina had seen what seemed to her a complete cycle of the Argentine political system. The anti-Peronist faction had won in 1955, sending Perón into exile and ushering in a series of military/semimilitary governments that vied for power and the public favor. Perón came back in 1973 to win democratic elections, and for the moment it seemed as if the country was set for a major change. However, with Perón's death a year later, the political stability began to falter, and newly formed guerrilla movements emerged, setting the stage for yet another anti-Peronist junta, on March 24, 1976, this time called the *Proceso de Reorganización Nacional* (Process of National Reorganization). For Catalina, much had happened in the last twenty years, but little had changed. As she says:

We were all afraid. I believe that there wasn't one Argentine that didn't have a little bit of this feeling, that wasn't afraid. I was afraid. I remember that when Julia Andrea was to be married in Buenos Aires, I spent the night with her in Córdoba in a house where Alberto, her future husband, lived. Alberto was on duty in the hospital. We slept in Córdoba so that we could go early the next day. We had to go to the hospital where Alberto was to look for the key to the car so that we could go. And we had a few blocks to walk. I believe that I never experienced such fear in my whole life as at that moment, afraid of coming across a police car that would see us. And I prayed that the police wouldn't show up until we had reached my son-in-law's hospital. Julia and I didn't speak of fear, neither of us, but I believe that we both felt the same.

Catalina still thanks God that they weren't taken away before reaching the hospital, that they made their way unharassed to Buenos Aires for the ceremony. It was a nice wedding, Catalina remembers, although she remembers being a bit upset that Julia was married by the justice of the peace instead of in a church. But those were different times, she admits, and in the end nothing went wrong. Relieved, Catalina returned to Córdoba, while the young couple made their way to the province of Neuquén, a mountainous region in southern Argentina, for their honeymoon.

Then the nightmare began. On June 3, that same year, while Julia and Alberto were still away on vacation, Julia's second-eldest brother, Luis Ignacio, was kidnapped by security forces of the Argentine government and presumably murdered, although his body was never found.

Catalina was devastated. Her youngest son was gone, and she didn't know why. There was no explanation for it, merely a brief phone call from a friend of Luis saying that he had been kidnapped. Catalina never saw him again. When Julia got word of her brother's disappearance, she quickly returned to La Fuente. When she saw Catalina she broke down crying. It was true, then, the rumors that were circulating about people who disappeared. It had finally touched their family. Julia stayed for a while with her mother, consoling her for several days, and then she and Alberto returned to Buenos Aires where they had recently moved.

Catalina was concerned about Julia's well-being. It didn't seem safe living in Buenos Aires. Julia told her mother not to worry. She and Alberto had traveled all the way from Buenos Aires to southern Argentina and back again; if they hadn't run into problems at any of the military checkpoints in all that distance, they had nothing to worry about. What had happened to Luis Ignacio was a tragedy, but it wouldn't happen to her, she said.

Catalina explains, "We saw Julia Andrea two days before they took her away. She had come to Carlos Paz" to where her mother and father had recently moved, "to collect her photographs from her honeymoon trip." There was another reason for Julia's visit. Before leaving her mother's house that day, March 4, 1977, Julia told her mother that she was two months pregnant. Catalina was gladdened by this last bit of news. At last, there was a sign that things would get better! As she said good-bye at the doorway, waving, Catalina could not know that she would never see that grandchild, nor would she ever see her only daughter alive again.

What happened next in the chain of events after Julia left her house that evening is not very clear for Catalina. She remembers that Julia was kidnapped March 6, while working in a clinic. She also knows that Julia's husband was kidnapped the same day. But the exact details of the moment, what she felt, where she went, all of it seems a whirl to her now, unreal, as if what was happening to her were a jumbled portrait of someone else's tragedy. She had lost two children now, and she still didn't know why. She tried to think of reasons. She knew that Luis Ignacio had been active as a union organizer, but was that reason enough for him to have been taken? And what of Julia? She was just a doctor. Was her last child in danger? Amid all this chaos and pain, the next point that Catalina's memory settles on is the one that remains fixed most clearly in her mind: her search for Julia.

As Catalina made haphazard inquiries at the local police stations, she heard so many conflicting stories that she didn't know what to believe. Some officials told her that it was solely a military matter, and she shouldn't get involved. Others said that Luis and Julia had most probably been the victims of some left-wing terrorist group. Still others denied that there had ever been any disappearances, and that they had really been "self-kidnappings" staged by revolutionaries to place blame on the military government.

Catalina didn't know who had taken her children. She didn't care. She just wanted them back. She wanted them alive. Her son, Manuel, tried to comfort her, saying, "Mamá, it's only going to be three, four months, before Julia is released." Looking back on that moment with tears in her eyes, Catalina now says, "I didn't think I could stand four months without my daughter."

As the months went by and Catalina made the rounds to the various human rights organizations, she began to realize that what she had been seeing before as her own suffering, her own personal pain, was actually the fate of a great many people. One evening, as she was attending a meeting to find out how to write letters to various government organizations, she was shocked to find that the information had been produced by a printing press instead of having been hand-typed or photocopied. She saw row upon row of gray folding tables stacked with mass-produced mimeographs, petitioning the then-President of the Junta Videla, the Organization of American States, and the United Nations. Catalina thought to herself, "It couldn't be that they'd send it to a printing press for just one or two people. There had to be a lot of us."

Catalina became more certain of this as she waited in the ever-growing lines outside the Ministry of the Interior, as she asked for information about her children. The mothers of the disappeared were told to take a number, as if they were waiting for turns in a delicatessen or in a bakery. It hardly seemed of any use to her. No one seemed to care. As she explains:

> They asked if I had information. Hey, I never had anything. And
> the last time that they assured me they were going to see about

my daughter's case, I went and they began to want to get information out of me. They didn't want to give me anything, but they wanted to get information, like with whom my son was living. I didn't know anything. I said that I'm not going to go anymore because the only thing they want to do is take information from me, and they're not going to give me any information.

If the security forces had taken her children, Catalina asked herself, why weren't her children listed as official prisoners in official jails? Why wouldn't the government give her any information? If her children were at least listed, although held incommunicado, it would have been easier to accept, but as she continued writing to all imaginable organizations, no one appeared to know anything. People just didn't disappear. And what about Julia's child? What crime did he or she commit? Were there facilities to take care of pregnant women? At this time, there was no talk of officially established concentration camps or torture chambers. Catalina did not know that the very people she patiently waited to talk to were already aware that her children were never coming back home.

Catalina found out in December of that year that the kidnapping had been carried out by members of the Argentine Armed Forces, and it had been part of an official operation. This confirmation came, not by way of the human rights groups, nor by way of the suspiciously silent Ministry of the Interior, but from the hierarchy of the Argentine Catholic Church. In her never-ending search for information, Catalina remembers someone telling her that there was a Catholic bishop who answered questions about people "who had been taken away."

This was Bishop Grasselli, a church official who had accepted the role of intercessor between the military government and family members of the disappeared. Grasselli had established himself in the Libertad building, the headquarters of the Armed Forces, and there, surrounded by soldiers, lines of mothers formed, waiting to ask a thousand questions about their missing children. Catalina remembers the day Grasselli received her.

We went to Libertad building and, well, they took our information and told us to come another time. I gave our documents, gave my identification. And the second time that we were there, they asked me about Luis. They said the revolutionaries changed names because they were involved in those things. They gave themselves other names; even their friends didn't know what they were called. And so they asked me if he was called I don't know what, and I told them that I only knew that he was called Luis Ignacio.

Bishop Grasselli said that he was unable to tell Catalina anything about her son, especially if she had nothing to tell him. However, he did have a list of a few prisoners that the military government had provided him, and this included Julia. As Catalina stated in her official testimony in 1983:

> Bishop Grasselli informed us in Libertad building, in an open way, and without any respect or shame, that my daughter and her husband were listed as detained up until June 17, 1977, giving us his interpretation that after that moment "the worst had happened" or "they were probably collaborating."

Catalina didn't understand what exactly the bishop was telling her. "What does this mean?" she asked. Grasselli looked at her across his desk and said slowly, "The Armed Forces either finished them, or they're collaborating, or they're working for them."

So Catalina had her answer, and she was terribly alone with the truth. "After that," she says, "we couldn't do anything else." Her family was irreparably split apart. Her government, her Church, had turned against her. Even those whom she had once considered friends became more and more distant, and soon they disappeared as well, afraid to be seen talking to this mother of subversives, to this trouble-maker.

When the lists of the officially recognized prisoners were published, Catalina went out and bought all the papers. When she didn't find Julia's or Luis's or Alberto's names in alphabetical order, she scanned the whole list in the hopes that the names had just been listed out of order. But as register after official register came out, none of the names appeared. The search for Luis ended with no further leads, and except for Bishop Grasselli's admission, no one connected with the Armed Forces, the police, or the government has ever admitted that Julia was ever imprisoned.

Because there were no fetal remains found in Julia's grave, the forensic anthropologists assured Catalina that Julia's child was born. Whether it was aborted naturally or, due to the conditions of the prison cells in which she was held, whether it was born dead or killed afterwards, or whether it was removed and placed in the home of a military family as many other children of the disappeared had been, is impossible to know. In the crowds of Buenos Aires, on the street, in the lines forming at bus stops, Catalina cannot be sure whether that seventeen year-old girl she sees, smiling as she remembers her young daughter smiling, is or is not her grandchild. As she scans the crowd, she cannot know if she should be looking for a girl or for a boy, and among so many faces she does not know where to begin.

Catalina's voice is almost inaudible as she finishes:

> For a while, we kept up hope, but afterwards one had hope, but it wasn't enough. It wasn't enough. Julia Andrea was a good person, and she didn't deserve this. The authorities told me at the beginning that, for me, my children were always good, but that perhaps, they really weren't. But I wanted the government to give them a trial, and to sentence them, but not to make them disappear, not that no one would ever do anything for them. Poor little ones.

Father Luis Angel Farinello

Priest at Nuestra Señora de Luján church in the city of
Quilmes, Buenos Aires; former third-world activist
known for his work in the field of social justice.

The role of the Catholic Church during the difficult years of the repression that we lived through was a fairly lamentable role, except for the very few of us bishops and priests that defended human rights. The majority didn't. It's a topic that didn't interest them very much. And more, I can tell you that in certain sectors of the Church, the military chaplains for example, they approved of the torture and disappearances of the people a bit. There was a theological basis that they gave to the military so that they could do these things without feeling guilty. There was a theology of death instead of Christ's doctrine that was always mercy, pardon, love, justice, truth. Christ, don't you see, was a victim. Jesus never killed anyone. He was the victim.

What barbarity it is that there were men of God, that there were sectors of the Church that in some way approved of all of this, or that hadn't done what was sufficient to make sure that this didn't happen, because if the Church in its entirety had been more valiant, many lives would have been saved!

You know that in the beginning the Church had its martyrs. The Christian was persecuted during the Roman Empire. When we didn't have power we were really persecuted, despised, in the Roman Coliseum. When we finally attained power, the power made us giddy and the Church burned at the stake how many thousands of people who didn't think like us? Look what power is, and through power we see what is black, white, and what is white, black. Because of this, we always say that power corrupts, no?

To be involved in diplomatic activities is very dangerous. Because, being in the center, with the power and with the people (and, well, if the people don't know if the information that they're giving will be misused later on), when you sit behind a desk being a diplomat, you're divided. And Christ wasn't divided. He clearly made his choice, because he was tortured and killed and poor, and he clearly chose a side. The world of diplomacy is the world of lies. Jesus didn't have anything to do with power. Since his birth in Bethlehem in a manger, simple and poor, until his death on the cross, which is the death of slaves, Jesus clearly chose his way of life. He didn't periodically visit the palace of Pilate or Caiphus. He never frequented those places. Only one time did Jesus enter the palace of Pontius Pilate. That was to be condemned to death. Nothing more. And, well, the Church, after Constantine, likes palaces, likes power, becomes the power and orders the death and torture by the inquisition of the people who didn't think like us. Terrible things. Terrible.

At that moment, the world had the look of profound change, didn't it? There was Che Guevara. Allende was in Chile. Perón was coming back to the country. There was Vatican II, where the Church began to open up, was changing Latin to Spanish, the organ to the guitar.

There was a great fervor in everyone. Kennedy was there, Khrushchev was in Russia. The Beatles, too, with their music. The hippies. They were the years of many changes. And so this served as well as a social and political change. We spoke of national socialism, and there was a generation of youngsters, of dreamers, and hippies, poets, those who showed solidarity, and they believed the world could change. Afterwards, one understood that they were, at best, very ingenuous. But with all of the goodness that comes from ingenuousness.

But we didn't realize that we were touching interests that were untouchable. And the repression was terrible. It was terrible. Because it wasn't just the guerrillas. The guerrillas, I don't know, were two thousand, three thousand; more than this would have been impossible or they would have done something else. The other victims were leaders from the neighborhoods, university representatives, catechism teachers, priests—nothing to do with violence, but the repression was brutal. Relatives, friends, because your name was in a letter all of these were targets—terrible atrocities were committed—including youngsters because they painted *Montoneros* on the street, at best without having a clear consciousness of what it was.

We're still paying the consequences of all those deaths, because all of these young people should be our leaders today. And, well, Argentina gave a lot of generous young people. Some were mistaken in the method, if you want; they chose violence. But what did we do so that they were violent? We defrauded them so many times with a cruel world, so treacherous and pharisaic. The other day I was saying that this democracy that we have in Argentina, now in all of the Americas, neoliberalism, all of the privatizations, destroys the people, and they don't have any work. We're fomenting a new violence, because in the long run democracy without justice brings violence. And if you sow winds you harvest storms. Injustice is being sown, immorality, corruption is being scattered about, and whom do people trust? The Church? The politicians? We're making the young people desperate.

In Argentina, there were priests like myself. I was part of the movement of the Third-World Priests. We were four hundred Argentine priests and eighteen bishops from the third world who sent a letter around the world [to the press, parts of the church, governments]. There were Filipinos and Brazilian bishops. They wrote a very beautiful letter about conditions in the third world. Then it occurred to us priests who thought like this to write a letter with our signatures, and, well, we were four hundred and we became excited and began to meet on a national level, and that's how the movement of the Third-World Priests arose. It was an experience in which we wanted to accompany the people. At this time, we asked the priests who were in this movement, all were worker-priests, priests who lived in poverty, that followed Jesus. We were all interested in social and political problems. And we were very abused. There were seventeen priests who were murdered by the military. Very close by was the murder of Father José Tedeski. They came to look for him on a Friday, at two o'clock in the afternoon, and we found his body at eleven o'clock at night in La Plata. Completely tortured. They had gouged out his eyes. They had cut off his penis. They had put his penis in his mouth.

And let's not just talk about the dead, but the prisoners as well. I, too, was a prisoner for a while. I was a prisoner in Rosario. I was accused of being a guerrilla and other things. The parish was surrounded many times by the military. They entered, looking for weapons. Here there were political/social activities. There weren't any political parties during the dictatorship. Well, I offered the church for many meetings. And this was a motive for their considering you a guerrilla or a leftist.

This is true. These years were very difficult, and all of us want to forget. Perhaps the only ones who don't want to forget are the Madres de la Plaza de Mayo (Mothers of the Plaza de Mayo). The politicians want to forget. "Punto final" (full stop), "obediencia debida" (due obedience), the pardon. The military wants to forget so that they can be free and so that the people will stop distrusting them, stop hating them. As a people, we don't have the dignity to stand up. Well, to tell you something, the retired people are calling for a just minimum wage, after having worked all of their lives, and many people pass them in the street and instead of giving them a look of compassion—or mercy—they continue straight on with their briefcases. Each one looks to save himself, and we don't have solidarity. This is terrible.

And there's a phrase that's pretty tough that I'm going to say to you: the Church that doesn't venerate its martyrs doesn't deserve to survive. And a people that doesn't venerate its generous young people, its tortured, I don't know if it deserves to survive. We're not one people. We don't have the minimum of dignity. I don't know. This is tough what I'm telling you. Terror paralyzes, but tell me, to what point have we sunk?

The military chaplains share one conception. They are more soldiers than they are priests. Do you know that there is a special seminary for those that are studying to be military chaplains? Yes, there's a seminary, so little by little they begin being formed specifically for this. And when a new military curate is to be named, it's not the Church who names him, who assigns a "great" priest that humanizes the military. No. The military has a lot to do with the nomination. If the priests don't think like them, then they don't accept them. Therefore, these chaplains, instead of teaching Jesus of Nazareth, they defend dogmas. They defend doctrine. Well, you have to save the fatherland, you have to save these Christian, Western values against the Marxist atheists, and I don't know what else. Therefore, in order to save the fatherland, anything goes. But this goes against Jesus of Nazareth. I believe that their great mistake is defending doctrine, defending "Western, Christian" values (within quotation marks), but they forget about Jesus of Nazareth.

The doctrine has to always be based on a person and that person is Jesus Christ, never on dogmas and on doctrine. If you defend doctrine, you end up not loving the person who thinks differently from you, when the first commandment is for all of us to love each other. And even love your enemy, Jesus says, kiss the feet of the enemy, as Jesus did before Judas, kneeling before him and washing his feet. So how can you torture a pregnant girl in the name of Jesus Christ? What, are we crazy? What deformity! What deformity, defending what values if we are stamping on the only great value, which is love?

They are like sick people. How is it possible that a boy such as the torturer Astíz has done what he has done? When did he enter the military academy? What book did they make him read? What type of brainwashing did they give him? And after giving this boy this sick mental education, on top of it all he ends up being proud of what he's done. Go and see what book he read, what education, what professors he had, what ideas, so that they can say that they were saving the fatherland and they were stealing children. I don't know, but it's bad education. It's the only explanation, like a sickness, that they brainwash you so that you're no longer a free person, conscious, who has grown, who chooses love. No. Now you're dependent on a terrible ideology that has made you see what is white, black.

My parish tends to many neighborhoods, slums. I serve at six chapels that we are constructing little by little. And in addition I have a day care center near the slum where every day eight hundred to nine hundred little kids eat. I have a maternity/child center. I have a cooperative housing center. I have a small factory where they make diapers and many things. I work with the poor people a lot.

Say "poverty" to the military and they think of you as a Marxist, of social classes, of the class struggle. Look, I spoke about this many times when I was in prison. They interrogated us, all of us first with violence, with rods. Afterwards, I spoke. But they're like that—blockheads. You think like them or you're the enemy. "I'm not a Marxist. I am a priest, and one of the things that Jesus says is 'blessed be the poor,' " the most elemental things in the gospel, and they don't understand them that way. Clearly, for them it is fomenting hatred between the rich and poor. It is also a way to bring cheer to the poor people so that they can organize, so that they discover their dignity, and this is a bother. It's convenient for the system in which we live that the people don't think.

When I gather food, a few clothes for the poor people, I'm a good priest—"What a good priest, how I must love the poor!" Now, when you look for the causes of the poverty, you begin to become a bother. When you say, "Hey, wait, every day I collect spaghetti or whatever and each time there are more poor people. Why? Why does this happen?" Then the government begins to think badly of you. You're not supposed to look for the causes, because if you do that, you want to change things, you want to overthrow the system. Now you're a subversive. When you say that this system doesn't work, this way, no, you have to subvert it, because this is not Christian, then the accusations come.

And, well, all Christians have to be subversives, because this is not the world that God dreamed about. Why produce weapons? Why do men have to give up their lives to weapons? When you say such a thing, they become upset, but, well, they are the subversives because they have put aside the order established by God, and they have made themselves powerful with money. One wants to return things to their normal state, with brotherhood.

We're still passing through the consequences of all of this horror. For now we should keep the memory alive somehow and remember the lost children and, moreover, to sow. I believe this is the moment to sow, in this same direction, but sowing. Still you can't see that little light of something different. We're really badly off. That little light that can draw together these utopias, these dreams, cannot be seen. It's a difficult moment. I think that we have to remember, and not forget, and at the same time sow, sow, devote our lives to sowing, and surely, because history doesn't end here, sprouts will grow. Lights will continue to ignite. The people will continue trying, and they will realize that this is not the first world, that this is not happiness, and well, disenchantment will come and young people will come, and we will begin to dream again and to grow. An alternative can't be seen yet, it can't be seen. But it will come. It's sure to come.

| | |

Graciela

Graciela says that she will always remember the day that Julia Andrea Montesini disappeared. That same day, March 6, 1977, Graciela's husband was electrocuted in an accident at work, leaving her to raise her three-year-old child alone. It was by the purest coincidence, Graciela says, that at the same time she lost the man she loved she also lost her closest childhood friend.

Long after the accident had occurred, she remembers talking to Julia's mother, Catalina, about the many emotions she felt at the loss of her husband. And she remembers thinking to herself, "It's different, the pain. At least, I know where he is." Without diminishing the loss of her husband, she could see that what had taken place that day were two different tragedies. Her husband's death was terrible; psychologically, emotionally, it was a painful experience. And yet, there was a certainty about it. Although bitter, there was a sense of completion, of a cycle coming to an end. There was none of this after Julia's disappearance. Julia was lost, presumed alive for the first few months, presumed dead for the many years afterwards, with no sense of surety until the day her remains were discovered. What was Julia other than a shadow that would reappear in her family's memories, in her own memories, half-alive, half-dead, haunting them?

After that terrible day, Graciela began to place distance between herself and the Montesini family, between herself and the subject of the disappeared. For the moment, she had to resolve her most immediate conflicts, work through her pain, and find a good way to raise her child. Afterwards, when she had let some time go by, she could begin to register that other loss, that other pain. In this way, she began to remember Julia.

Graciela recalls the first day she met Julia in grammar school in the village of Pilar de la Sierra:

> We entered first grade together in the same school. I wasn't familiar with anything there because I lived in the countryside. I didn't have any friends from before. And at school, I began to find my way around. (These are things that happen to you when you are a kid.) And well, really, I don't remember how it was, but among the group of children I began to talk more with her, Julia Andrea, than with the other girls. For sure, I went first to Julia's house before she went to mine. I was an only child. Going to her house with three children was more fun for me. And she preferred coming to my house because you could be alone, and no one bothered you.

The two young girls attended El Instituto Nuestra Señora de Pilar, a private Catholic school run by nuns who, Graciela recalls, were quite strict. The original school building still stands, just off the tree-lined main square of Pilar de la Sierra, and it's still open to the children of the village. It is run by lay teachers now, however, instead of nuns, who were forced out of the village during the 1970s after having been accused of spreading communist literature. With a smile, Graciela says she doesn't know whether that meant teaching the Bible or not.

It was a financially accessible school that received partial state support. Each child paid a basic fee to go to Nuestra Señora de Pilar, but it was low enough so that everyone who wanted to could go. It was a healthy atmosphere, she remembers, with children from different social classes, the landowning elites, the poor children on the outskirts of town, the small middle class.

Graciela remembers the year that she and Julia won a trip to the resort town of Mar de Plata for having the highest grade point averages in the school. They were twelve years old, and it remains one of Graciela's fondest memories of time spent with Julia. She still doesn't know how her parents ever let her go, she says. Of course, the trip was supervised by a group of nuns, but a few boys from nearby schools who had also won were allowed to go with them as well. Boys on a trip with the girls from Nuestra Señora de Pilar? An almost impossible thought!

Graciela tries to make little of her academic record. She says that winning the trip was not so much due to her own intelligence as to the terribly low averages of the rest of the students. She didn't even try, she says. For her, school was boring, especially gym. Graciela doesn't believe there was a single Argentine child at the time who really liked gym. As for Julia, she wasn't

> the very studious child who kept herself separated from the rest. She was very intelligent, very quick, especially in mathematics, logic games. She would always laugh and say, "You like all of those subjects that have to do with language, literature, poems. Do them for me, and I'll do your math problems" because counting wasn't difficult for her at all. But I would say about math, "Explain this to me, how do you do this? Because it looks like Chinese." Since recitations or subjects that had to do with languages weren't difficult for me, we used to exchange homework.

Although Julia wasn't one for literature when it was forced on her at school, she enjoyed reading in her spare time. Her favorite book was *The Little Prince*. After she had read it, she was so moved by the poetry and the figure of the boy that she gave her copy to Graciela so she could read it. That was how Julia was, Graciela says, honest in what she felt, uninhibited. As Graciela tries to describe Julia, she remembers

> one summer in February, it was ten degrees Celsius, the year that I turned fifteen. And I tell you, we were all going around in sweaters, and it was sleeting, you see. More than rain, it was snow that fell that day, which was extremely strange. We were in the countryside, and we were going to have a party. There was a swimming pool, and a man was going to come and film us, to take pictures of the moment. He supposed that we would be dying of the heat. It was, I'm telling you, almost snowing. And because he had set up everything and was there with his equipment, Julia Andrea put on her bathing suit and jumped into the water. I wouldn't do that, not even if I were crazy. In the water. And she put on a face of being hot, in order to go with the filming. I want to tell you that she was a person who wasn't going to be scared by anything. She had fun. I don't know. She was a very positive person.

Graciela understands that every adolescent girl goes through periods of personal doubt and agony over who she is, if she's ugly or not, what her friends think of her, if her clothing is acceptable, and she assumes that Julia must have been the same. But if she were, Julia didn't seem to show it. She relied more on herself and her own opinions than those of the crowd. "I believe that Julia Andrea was always a leader," Graciela explains, "because ever since primary school, for example, she was the girl that made decisions. She didn't order people about, but her opinions always held weight."

Graciela says that the word that best describes the social life in Pilar de la Sierra when she was growing up is "boring." Although Pilar had all the advantages of a small town, the fresh air, the animals, the close relationships that formed between the neighbors, "if you didn't look for something to do, more than your homework, it was boring." It was not Buenos Aires, with its pubs and cafés and row upon row of movie theaters. And it's not like nowadays, Graciela says, with young girls running off in their miniskirts at all hours of the night to cheap discotheques, or *boliches* as they are called. In Pilar, the closest the children ever got to discothéques was having parties at houses of friends, while their parents looked on from the kitchen.

> And everyone brought something to eat or to drink, because the party was pretty much improvised from one day to the next. So each one of us brought something, and we called these "assaults." My father could never understand. It sounded ugly to him. An assault is something bad, so he never let me host one. We danced separately because this was the time of rock and roll, the twist. You danced to tropical music too, which later came back into fashion, the *cumbe*, all of this. But afterwards, we played slow songs, *boleros*, by Los Panchos and the rest. And all of a sudden you were going steady for having danced extremely close with someone. Clearly. Yes. Listen, you fell in love like a lunatic. At best, it was your neighbor whom you had seen every day for all of your life, but aah, you discovered him at the dance. It was something like that.

Graciela remembers her adolescence as being an extremely beautiful although extremely ordered stage of her life. Rock and roll might have come to Pilar de la Sierra, but little else from the sixties seemed to have made it. Her daughter, now a teenager herself, laughs when she sees her mother's old photographs, the long, formal dresses, and the highly stylized hairdos. Illegal drugs were completely unknown, Graciela says, and the sexual revolution was likewise decades behind. There were quite a number of boys who drank alcohol to excess in order to purge the boredom of village life, but it was not acceptable for a girl to do the same. For Graciela and her friends, there were few routes open to rebel against the system. Graciela chose smoking. She thinks she was about seventeen when she began, "but never in my house," she says. "I was a rebel, but outside. And eating breath mints or something afterwards to cover up the smell. And Julia Andrea as well. We'd get together, and we'd be chatting for a little while, and then we began smoking. And when we were studying. The majority smoked, and so we smoked. Not because we liked it, but because everyone smoked."

These two girls, similar in many ways, had different dreams of how they would escape small-town life. Graciela was very clear that she would leave Pilar, marry, and raise a family. Julia, too, wanted a family, and Graciela remembers their conversations, as they walked in the countryside or rode horses at her father's farm, deciding how many children they were going to have, three, four, five. . . . But above all, Julia wanted to become a doctor. And pursuing medicine wasn't just a career decision for her, Graciela insists. It was a way of life. For Julia it seemed the proper synthesis of all that she had ever learned, from her parents, from the nuns at school, from the sense of community in Pilar. As Graciela explains:

> In our houses, our home, the most essential thing was not politics. I think that the most important idea was to show solidarity, to help. Julia Andrea, for example, studied for her teaching certificate in high school, and the idea was to pursue medicine, to work as a teacher, and to follow medicine. She always had an extremely clear vision, not to be the doctor who sets up a private practice here, earns a lot of money, buys some land, and afterward lives well. Not that. Nothing to do with it. To work in a hospital, to improve the hospital locally, I suppose, with better care. That is to say, she was always for the social part, for helping the people.

Graciela remembers that one of Julia's older brothers, Luis Ignacio, had clear ideas about what he wanted from the future as well, but he was different from Julia, more political, more radical. Julia's dreams seemed to depend on helping the people where they were today, focusing on their needs, without a concern for their politics. Luis Ignacio's plan was to show them another way by challenging the structure of Argentine society:

> Luis Ignacio was the child before Julia Andrea, a boy who didn't study, who went away from here to work and became involved in

union activities. He had political pamphlets in his house at this time. And he used to poke fun at me because, for him, I was part of the bourgeoisie, because I had farmland, the "cattle oligarchy" as it used to be called at this time. In Argentina years ago, it was believed that the people who had farmland were very powerful, had a lot of money. So he would always say to me as a joke that we had, I'm not telling you slaves, but in a way that we lived off of the people, that we didn't pay them well and this sort of thing. He was middle-left, and he knew that I never had anything to do with this, no political ideas at all, except ideas of liberty and justice, but concerning organized parties, nothing. So he always used to poke fun at me. He was a little like a brother to me. They were all my brothers and sister.

Graciela recalls the divided political atmosphere in which she and the other Argentines in her generation grew up. She remembers, when she studied biology and agronomy in Buenos Aires, being frightened by the rallies of the right-wing parties, those that represented a venomous nationalism, mixing the business interests and those of the landed aristocracy with slogans such as "Argentina for the Argentines," almost a "Nazi" movement, Graciela says. The discontented mass, repelled by the brutal rhetoric of the nationalists, became intrigued by the intellectual vanguard of poets, musicians, unionists, and educators who settled toward the left. It became fashionable to become a leftist. Graciela heard a lot of talk about utopias and social progress, but she didn't see much action. Graciela felt that little choice existed other than these two distinct movements, and at eighteen years old the average Argentine was inevitably pressed into the mold of one philosophy or the other.

Graciela thinks that the left went wrong when it tried to translate its rainbow of ideals and dreams into action. From its position in the clouds, talk of an armed struggle against what it considered a static, militaristic society might have seemed quite rational and just, but when some groups began taking hostages, robbing banks, beginning an armed insurrection in the north, the dream collapsed into anarchy. Graciela remembers:

Julia Andrea told me, "Luis is getting involved in something, he's become involved in a situation that's not going to come to anything good." He had gotten involved in the political side of the Peronist Party, the part on the left, that was the most committed part. The first that was going to be broken. That is to say, it was very evident that they were progressing a bit, and it wasn't only ideological, but rather they were acting. And I talked about this with Julia Andrea, and she had nothing to do with this. She never helped her brother. According to what she told me, it didn't seem like anything good to her, or for Luis, to compromise himself, compromise his family more each time.

Months after Julia's disappearance, Graciela contacted the Montesini family. She hadn't heard from them for a long time, and she was happy to hear Catalina's voice again. But Catalina was afraid. She said, "Don't come to see us anymore, because I don't know if Julia had your address in some notebook, and they're going to come looking for you. You've got a baby girl, so take care of yourself, take care."

Graciela was confused by what Catalina said. She had never felt afraid for herself or her child. She had never been involved in politics, so she didn't see why she should maintain her distance from the Montesinis. Anyway, such a long time had gone by since Julia's disappearance that she thought if the military hadn't come looking for her by now, they never would.

Graciela still doesn't know what to make of all that went on. Disjointed and contradictory rumors reached the people in Pilar de la Sierra, and the channels of communication were so controlled by the military that Graciela didn't know what information to accept and what to discard. One story was that Julia had been transferred to a jail in Misiones, one of the northern provinces, and that she had given birth to a baby boy. Another rumor was that a pregnant woman from Pilar (presumably Julia) had been sighted briefly in a detention center in the south. None of these stories have ever been confirmed or denied.

Even today, many different versions of Julia's story make their rounds through the village. "I don't know if we're cured [of this misinformation]," Graciela says. She points to the experience of the Malvinas/Falklands war in which the majority of Argentines supported armed conflict against Great Britain, believing that they were winning up until the ultimate victory of British forces. "Because I tell you, we were convinced about the Malvinas, we were convinced that the islands had to be ours. I almost went as a volunteer nurse for example. They convince you easily."

After the horrors of the Dirty War had come to light in the trials of the Junta members in 1985, Graciela realized how many people had been taken away "without a reason," and she began seriously to doubt that Julia had been involved in anything close to the guerrilla movements. "She was either at home, or she was in the hospital. And she didn't have any time for that. This is what really makes me think that she really wasn't very involved." Yes, she might have followed her brother when he went to political rallies, or she could have fallen in with the wrong crowd at the university, but Julia's personality, her philosophy, seemed to renounce violence. Her vocation was to save lives, not to take them.

Looking back on all that has happened since that March day so many years ago, Graciela says it's difficult to describe what she feels. The pain that she suffered in losing Julia is different from that of losing her husband. It's not worse. It's not less. It's just different. "It was a difficult moment," she says. "I believe that it marked all of us. I believe that it's a whole generation that has been marked."

Life continues for Graciela in Pilar de la Sierra. She now lives with her parents and her daughter in a house in town, and, for a few months out of the year, she goes to her parents' farm to be with the horses and the sheep that she once devoted so much time to as a child. And sometimes, when she's walking in the countryside, down the trails, through the pastures on the outskirts of the village, she remembers the young, vivacious girl who used to accompany her. Sometimes it makes her sad. Sometimes she laughs, remembering the dances, the swimming pool, the hidden cigarettes, all of the things that she and Julia once did together. It's enough for Graciela to remember now, enough for her to remember Julia, how she dressed, how she smiled, and then she goes on.

VOICE 3

Dr. Ester Saavedra

*Psychologist and therapist for family members of
disappeared people and of victims of the military
repression.*

I am part of the same generation as the majority of the disappeared,
and I was involved in political activity in school at that time. When
the dictatorship obliged you to withdraw a bit, we psychologists all
worked in fairly private places, not in public, making a career of solidarity among the victims of the people we knew, friends, family members, mothers. But when it became public we formed an assistance
group. During the years before our work was made public, I attended
to people in a private practice.

Sometimes people came just because they guessed that they could
trust you, that you wouldn't turn them in, and that you were going to

understand. These were the two key things: security and understanding a great dimension of horror that the people lived through, the threat of disappearing, not just the dimension of the loss of a friend or a relative, a cousin, a brother, but living with the fact that they also could disappear.

The disappeared person is a very particular entity. In 1976 the people who talked about the people who had been taken away said, "They took him away." They couldn't say, "He's a *desaparecido*." It was, "My friends are no longer here." I remember what one young kid who was doing his military service at the time said: "I'm afraid. My friends are no longer here. Some left, some were taken away." That was as much as he was able to say, and he never could talk about where he supposed his friends were. He knew that I was more or less trustworthy but, all the same, no one got up the courage to talk. "What is a *desaparecido?*" It is something very particular because it's a person who's missing but someone you need, for emotional reasons—and sometimes for political reasons—to make present. It's very particular.

It's a missing person whose absence one doesn't want to be made an accomplice to. This would be equivalent to decreeing the disappearance, decreeing the death of the loved one. That is what is so difficult for the family members; because of the hatred they feel for having had their child taken away, that he's been kidnapped, they can't say that he's dead. That's what makes it very particular. On the other hand, it's the uncertainty of death, the question that there's no exact proof, no ashes, no bones. This makes the disappeared person into a type of living-dead, and like the experiences that primitive peoples talk about, of flying saucers or the men who return, it's often quite present in fantasy. Moreover, these fantasies can return from a place such as social death because the disappeared person has been taken away from the community, but, moreover, he might return after having passed through an experience of torture, et cetera, and that's the image that they're afraid to find.

There are many family members who say, "He showed up! I passed him in the street." I remember a mother who believed that her son was living on the floor above her apartment. I didn't believe it. I say that this was madness, but all the same she said, "I saw him leaving the other day, and he's exactly the same. Could it be he?"

I believe that the definitive death opens the road to being able to connect yourself with that which continues to live. Because you know that this person is not around anymore, and that, although he's been murdered, you can at least say they killed him—"It was so and so who killed him" or "We're investigating who killed him." Death is the certainty that the person will not come back to life. The disappeared person is always a promise that he can still be around. That's why I believe in the term living-dead, because it's someone who's dead because you can say, "He can't be alive," but on the other hand it doesn't give you the certainty that he is dead. He wasn't buried.

In our culture we bury the dead underground because there's a necessity to distance life and death in order to continue to live. And well, with the disappeared people, you can't do that. Then, they're like phantoms, no? They are, I believe, that image from classical theatre, of phantoms that wander because they don't have a resting place or because there are crimes that condemn them.

I believe that there is no rest for those that are the living while there is no type of social distance. This is very important for us, because, although the bones show up, this particular situation doesn't end because of the way in which the person was disappeared. Look, in the case of Julia Montesini, the question of whether she had a child comes up again. The possible return appears. Moreover, there's no social agreement over how it occurred, nor is there punishment for what the military did. Then this makes it impossible for the grief to be normal. This grief can't be normal; it's not the loss of anyone, the death of anyone.

I believe that the great majority of the people during the dictatorship who didn't have news about what was going on didn't want to have it. I can tell you that there were thousands of moments when we knew what was going on. We saw the people from the Organization of American States, saw the line of people. And I remember the club where my husband used to go. I brought this up there, and some of them said, "Ah, these people are just making a lot of trouble." Then, you'd say, "No, listen, it's certain that they're taking people away," and they'd say, "Ah, please, what is there to do?"

You felt that there was a need to believe the official version because it was too painful to suppose that there were disappearances, that people had been kidnapped, while we were living a normal life. We lived a brazen life. It wasn't Chile. We didn't have a curfew with everyone stuck in his house. The dollar was cheap, and we spent our life traveling, as if everyone was saying, "Nothing's happening here." There was a coexistence of one life that pretended to be completely normal and organized and peaceful. That was very difficult to take. I believe that this generated guilt, the mechanism of defense and denial. The mechanism of defense and denial was what happened at the beginning. Afterward, they couldn't deny it, but still they tried to forget because when they forgot that it happened they could pretend to resolve conflicts that weren't resolved.

There are people who falsify history, who invent another history, in order not to remain with the feelings of guilt, or in order not to feel dragged down by the destiny of the other. That is to say, not to be contaminated by the destiny of the other. There are people who need to feel that they don't have anything to do with this person. The terror generated this because all of us had contact with the people who disappeared. The dictatorship was telling you that if you were a friend of this guy who was taken away, you could be taken away as well. But it's a question that unconsciously we all have, like with someone who has AIDS. People don't want to get close although they know that they're not going to get the disease. That which is socially stigmatized is sickness or death, disappearance or even political activism.

We had group meetings with people who are in the university now in order to discuss how they lived through this, how they processed it. They have blank spaces. They get up the courage to formulate questions in the group: "Yes, I wanted to ask my mother why she didn't tell me why she took me by the hand to school, why she didn't let me come home late at night, didn't let me go out to dance. Why didn't they tell me what was going on?" And sometimes with anger and rage because if they didn't tell them, they were accomplices in a way. It's something very painful, very difficult to remove. And this, in general, the people negated, not wanting to know.

I believe that the disappeared person brings something that disturbs the natural order of things, disturbs life, that remains fixed in the place of the disappeared person. Because people just don't disappear. They can die of a disease or they can be killed, in war or by murder, but they do not disappear. This word *desaparecido* brings with it something of the supernatural order. This leaves a type of hole, a type of black hole, you see? Many times, what I have seen is that the disappeared person takes, let's say, symbolically, many parts of other people.

There are people who have been left behind as detainees, as if they had been taken away instead of the other, as the effect of having a disappeared person in their life. I believe that there is a lot of this that sucks away vital aspects of the people who were left behind, as prisoners. I have attended to families that for ten years did not celebrate New Years' or a birthday. I attended to one family that never celebrated the birthday of the children after one of the sisters disappeared. It was a guilt that meant life shouldn't continue its course. They had to stop life. So they didn't celebrate rituals—the rituals in our culture, birthdays—as if they could deny that it ever happened. And when the older sister graduated from high school and began at the university, she received a sudden jolt, because how could this happen? It was as if nothing could continue its course. The mother wouldn't allow the wedding of one of the girls who was going to get married because there was a resistance, as if a part of them had to disappear.

If you speak with a mother of a disappeared person, many times she's going to tell you, "Because Julia is. . . ." and you're to see how she makes her present, something that happens many times when someone dies and you speak about the person in the present tense for about fifteen days. Afterwards, you begin to speak about the person in the past. Or she'll say, "My son would be this tall, would be this old." She can't say, "My son was this old when he was taken away." She speaks about how many years old he would be today. To say, "I remember" and to have all the memories that he isn't here is very painful. Moreover, it's painful not only because it registers the absence, but also because it's the ones who survived who are the ones to decide that they can start talking about so and so in the past, and this is an act to which a lot of guilt is attached. I believe that Manuel could say it because he buried Julia, and it appears to me that the burial gave him a type of forgiveness. Now he can remember her in a different way.

I V

Manuel

Manuel doesn't know where he first heard the word, but he remembers being so terrified that he might become one that he ran to the village priest. There, kneeling in the confessional box, eight years old, Manuel confessed that he secretly feared he would become a "communist." But what did it mean? The priest said that the matter was entirely out of his hands and that the little boy had to wait for the Jesuits to decide. Manuel agonized for weeks until the Jesuit group that traveled from village to village giving catechism classes finally arrived. He went directly to one of the young priests and unburdened himself with his sin. The priest burst out laughing and told him that he wasn't to blame, that he shouldn't worry himself about such big words until he was older. Manuel left, confused, but feeling better.

Manuel remembers his childhood in the village of Pilar de la Sierra as relatively peaceful, far from the mainstream of Argentine political life. It was, in fact, a world apart. When he visited his grandparents in nearby La Fuente, he remembers his grandmother hushing him and whisking him out of the living room so that she could listen to *News of the World* on the wireless, an hour-long résumé of great world events, news from England and Italy. And that was all. Once a day for an hour the world opened up in La Fuente, and then it closed again, and village life resumed its normal indifference to outside events. Nothing ever seemed to happen there, Manuel remembers.

Manuel feels quite sure that his parents knew what was going on outside the village, but he himself passed through the apex of President Perón's power in the late 1940s, the revolution of 1955 that unseated him, and the fits and starts of military and civilian rule for years afterwards, in relative ignorance. As he says:

> I suppose my family knew who was governing at the time—of course, they did—but I didn't. Our educational system here is absolutely terrible. That is to say, they taught me who San Martín was, and how many warts he had on each foot, but nothing really more than that. And it's possible that I could be studying this and not know what president was governing me.

There was one political maxim, however, with which Manuel was extremely familiar—"Never be a Peronist." This was not a lesson learned from school but rather a commandment from his father, a virulent anti-Peronist. It was quite an iconoclastic stance for the 1950s, considering that Perón seemed to reach in and dominate every aspect of Argentine life. In studying the alphabet, children's grammar books often began with "E" instead of "A," for president Perón's socially charming and politically powerful second wife, Eva "Evita" Duarte. Children would say their prayers at night for Evita and for General Perón, and then for their own mothers and fathers, in the order that the Peronist regime preferred. Manuel remembers having to write an essay on Evita's autobiography, *The Reason for My Life*, in order to enter secondary school.

Regardless of the overwhelming pressure to be otherwise, the Montesini family was anti-Peronist, and there was no doubting it. When

Perón was finally overthrown in 1955, Mr. Montesini reveled in it. For good or bad, another military government had taken over, but at least Perón was gone. Manuel explains:

> My generation was taught that way. They taught us all of the "anti's," anti-Peronism, anti-that. But that it was necessary to participate in order for things to be different, this was never part of my generation. We weren't doing anything, because they taught us not to participate. I believe that it's a generational blame. Of course, you're going to find a lot of people my age who are going to tell you that they were politically active, but it wasn't that way in my case.

In the 1960s, Manuel burst out of Pilar de la Sierra and into the wide political world of Córdoba, the capital of the province by the same name, where he traveled to study architecture. It was certainly different from the few scattered bits of information that he eavesdropped from his grandmother's news program. There were small demonstrations and political talks in the parks about the condition of the nation, the new political system, and, more importantly, there were people who listened. For a brief time, Manuel returned to live with his parents, homesick and tired of studying arches and buttresses. But he knew that he couldn't stay in Pilar forever, so he went back to Córdoba, this time in order to study medicine.

It was in Córdoba that Manuel became interested in politics and started attending demonstrations together with his little sister Julia, who by now was studying medicine as well. He explains that, at first,

> I wasn't very active. I used to go to the student demonstrations but I was afraid because the police showed up on horseback. And every time I wanted to go, and I went with Julia Andrea, I ended up scared to death on seeing the first horse running. Sometimes we would get separated, and Julia Andrea would forget what cafeteria she had planned to meet me in afterwards.

As Manuel slowly moved along the political margin of Córdoba, apprehensive of getting involved and quite afraid of horses, his brother Luis Ignacio threw his old family education aside and thoroughly embraced, of all things, Peronism. In the successive shuffling of semi-democratic/military governments of the 1950s and 1960s, Argentine youth became extremely disenchanted with the establishment, a disenchantment that gave birth to the idea that the only solution was for ex-President Perón to return from exile, deus ex machina, and permanently rid the country of its many problems, from corruption to social injustice.

Manuel remembers the city filled with posters, tie-dyed shirts, and students singing protest songs. The Vietnam War was at its climax, and Córdoba was alive with its own brand of flower power, seeing in its military government a reflection of the "imperialistic" United States of America. It was Luis who was always in front, marching, protesting, organizing rallies, and Manuel remembers that it was Julia who always went with him. She followed him everywhere, Manuel recalls, always his shadow, his number one supporter. She never seemed to pronounce a political plan of her own, never raised her voice, never seemed to direct the flow of events, but she followed, and she would do anything for Luis Ignacio.

It was this close contact with her brother that would soon place both Julia and the entire Montesini family in great danger.

Perón returned to power in June 1973 and died little more than a year later, without having fulfilled the dreams of the insistent Argentine youth. María Estela Martínez (known as Isabelita), Perón's third wife, assumed the presidency, and as she did, all across Argentina the long shadow of dictatorship could be seen approaching.

What followed Maria Estela's assumption of power was close to the total breakdown of Argentine society. Right-wing death squads roamed freely, killing and torturing people at will. Leftist rebels switched from their positions of kidnapping and extortion of rich businessmen to placing bombs in movie theaters and supermarkets. No one's security could be assured, the economy was failing, and, as the Peronist ball of string began to unwind rapidly, Isabelita found that she did not have the power to put a stop to it.

The night of May 13, 1975, Manuel was at home in Pilar de la

Sierra, watching television. Julia was laid up in bed, sick with the flu. Suddenly a group of eight to ten young men dressed in civilian clothes burst into their house, pointing machine guns at them. They menaced the entire family, threatening to kill them if they didn't tell them where Luis Ignacio was. They especially terrorized Manuel, demanding to know the names of any friends of his brother. Manuel's mind went completely blank. He was terrified and couldn't remember any names at all, not one. Finally a name came tumbling out: "el Chivo," he thought he might have remembered, but he couldn't be sure. Satisfied with this answer, the paramilitary group sacked the house, carrying off whatever they could.

Manuel went to the local police station to file a *denuncia*, or complaint, about the sacking of his house. The commissioner took Manuel aside and told him off the record that the squad had been formed from personnel from the Federal Police. Police from that very police station had been instructed not to interfere with the "proceedings." What would later be described as a "free zone" or "green light" had been established in the Montesini's neighborhood, meaning that the military informed the local police they were not to get involved, were not to answer the calls for help from frantic neighbors, as their houses were sacked or their children assassinated.

On March 24, 1976, the three branches of the Argentine Armed Forces overthrew president María Estela Martínez de Perón, establishing a junta known as the Process for National Reorganization, or *el Proceso de Reorganización Nacional.* Early that morning, at the automobile factory where Luis Ignacio was a union organizer, the six o'clock shift was rounded up and taken away by soldiers. It was part of *el Proceso*'s economic goals to "reorganize" the highly Peronist unions, completely to make them fall in line with the austere plans of the new economic minister Martínez de Hoz. This new government preferred to implement the reorganization by murdering the union organizers or making them disappear, thus establishing a right-wing management more to their liking. Luis Ignacio did not show up as scheduled for the nine o'clock shift and immediately went underground.

After the coup, life for the Montesini children, as for all of Argentina, underwent a drastic change.

Manuel remembers visiting Julia and her fiancé, Alberto Espinoza, in Córdoba later that year to help them get some items out of storage. They made a bonfire behind the house, burning everything that might be considered subversive by the dictatorship. They did not have anything obvious, like posters of Che Guevara or copies of *Das Kapital*, but they burned rock and folk records and (which Manuel most regrets), Pablo Neruda's poetry, old letters, photographs of anyone who might have been thought to be a revolutionary or who had disappeared.

After destroying the incriminating evidence of their youth, they went inside their house to have spaghetti. There was a tension in the air, as the fire burned down outside, and they sat eating in silence. Then, as Manuel remembers:

> Alberto said that he wanted to tell me that he and Julia had decided to cut all ties they had with Luis. And I told him that I really didn't understand, that they had decided to totally cut all ties with Luis? I didn't understand. I didn't understand. "How can this be, Julia?" Julia didn't answer. She only cried.

Manuel couldn't understand why Julia had abandoned her brother out of what appeared to be fear, especially now when he needed her most. What had changed her so much?

Alberto said that it was too dangerous for Julia to have any contact with Luis. It was bad enough what had happened in 1975 to their house in Córdoba, but that was under a civilian government. What would happen now in the middle of a military dictatorship? Because of this argument and other personal conflicts regarding Luis, Manuel did not attend the wedding of Alberto and Julia on May 18, 1976.

Soon after Luis Ignacio had been kidnapped, Manuel remembers talking to Julia, trying to convince her not to go to Buenos Aires as she had planned, that the big, turbulent city wasn't safe for her. She should move away from all the excitement and, like the family had done, go to Villa Carlos Paz, still in the Province of Córdoba, especially now that Luis Ignacio was gone. But Julia wouldn't listen. They hadn't done anything wrong, she said, and they didn't deserve to live in fear. Wasn't it their right to be happy? She'd move to Buenos Aires and stay there until Alberto finished his internship in cardiology, and then she would follow him south to buy a house, and then they would start a family.

After Luis was kidnapped, Manuel had gone to Buenos Aires, searching frantically from one human rights group to another, to government agencies, church groups, asking the same questions: Did anyone know anything about his brother? Who had taken him? Was it the police, the Armed Forces, or one of its myriad intelligence branches? He just wanted a few words, a promise that he was alive. A Methodist group taught him how to make a declaration of habeas corpus, how and where to send telegrams, in his attempt to climb rung after rung in the Junta's bureaucracy. Manuel learned how to switch from buses to taxis, circle the buildings he would enter before going in to make sure he wasn't being followed.

Looking back on these terrible days of fear and doubt, the dates blend together for Manuel. It was either March 5 or 6, 1977, that he went to La Liga Argentina para los Derechos Humanos (The Argentine Human Rights League), an organization initially created in the time of Perón to defend members of the Communist Party. Manuel sat down among the Communists, years away now from the confessional box in Pilar de la Sierra, and began to explain his story to a young man who worked there. As he recounted his bits of scattered information, the man interrupted, saying,

"If they took your brother, then you've got to leave the city."

"But why?" he said. "My brother was a union delegate. They were looking for him. I have a sister living in Buenos Aires, and nothing's happened to her."

The man looked at him seriously and said, "Nothing's happened to her—yet. Look, don't sleep in your house tonight. Your parents can do what they want, but I'm telling you, they're taking entire families."

Manuel left the League terrified and confused. He hadn't done anything. Luis Ignacio had always been the target. And what of Julia . . . ?

He hurried back to Carlos Paz. On the long way home by bus, he kept thinking of ways to make his sister leave Buenos Aires. How stubborn she'd been! What could he say to make her leave? What were the right words that would convince her? But more immediately, whatever happened to Julia, Manuel had to find a safe place to spend the night. It was necessary but difficult for the family, as Manuel recalls:

> My father had family, but they weren't really close. At this time, there was little help because of the great amount of fear. My mother took it badly. "Why do you have to keep escaping? What have we done?"

His parents decided that Manuel should spend the night at his aunt's house close by. His aunt was reluctant to take him in, not wanting to become involved in something that she shouldn't be, but she finally agreed. Late that night, most probably March 6, the telephone rang in his aunt's house. It was Julia's friend, Laura. She had called the aunt's house because there was no phone in the Montesini home and she had reached Manuel by chance.

"Look, I'm calling you because I can't go over there," Laura said. "But you have to know what's happened."

"What happened?" Manuel asked, suddenly awake.

"They 'interned' Julia and Alberto."

"What? Are they sick?"

"No. No. . . they have the same illness as Luis Ignacio."

Manuel hung up and ran to his room, getting dressed as quickly as possible. He had understood Laura's code. It wasn't safe to talk on the telephone. The worst had happened: Julia and Alberto had been disappeared as well. But how had it happened? Why? He had to get back to his parents' house and see if they were all right. He hurried out the door.

When Manuel arrived back at his house, he found his parents discussing the situation nervously with Alberto's father. Someone had told him of his son's disappearance, and he had come to the Montesinis, hoping for further news. Although the information was still muddled at the time, Manuel learned that Julia had been kidnapped while on night shift at the clinic of Nuestra Señora de Luján in the city of Lomas de Zamora, just outside of Buenos Aires. An hour afterwards, her husband Alberto had been seized in the group house where they were living in Buenos Aires. It was later learned that everyone in the group house had been taken away with Alberto, including the mother of one of the students living there. Some were brutally beaten by the soldiers who took them. All of those taken were released except for Alberto, who was never seen again.

The next day, what was left of the Montesini family went into hiding. Manuel and his parents stayed with friends until they could book passage out of Villa Carlos Paz, and then, under cover of darkness, they took the train to the northern province of Jujuy, where Manuel spent the next eleven months hiding at a relative's house, not knowing where Julia was and living in dread that the soldiers would come knocking at his door as well.

At the end of 1977, Manuel and his parents returned to Villa Carlos Paz. Fearing the worst if he went back to Córdoba to finish his studies, he began to work instead at a series of odd jobs, supporting himself and his parents as well. Manuel began his life again, older now and without a college degree. His country was still in the middle of the dictatorship, and he was alone, without Julia, without Luis. He lived this way for the next five years until the end of *el Proceso*, working as a clerk in a small clinic where once he might have been the doctor. In the wake of the overwhelming Argentine military defeat that ended the Malvinas/Falklands War, the Armed Forces reluctantly allowed democracy to return in 1983. At this time, Manuel began to publish small articles in the local newspapers, send taped messages to radio stations, and make the rounds to the nascent human rights organizations, Mothers of the Plaza de Mayo and Grandmothers of the Plaza de Mayo. He asked if anyone had seen Julia, if anyone had any information at all. Although there were no answers, he took comfort in the fact that he was not alone in his pain: an estimated thirty thousand men, women, and children had disappeared.

Then, one day he received a phone call from the Argentine Forensic

Anthropology Team, telling him that it was possible that they had identified his sister. That night he cried, "Dear God, could it finally be over?" He says:

> After finding the remains of Julia Andrea, I went to spend a few days in the house of my cousin. My cousin's wife asked me, "Do you need me to go to Julia's funeral?"
>
> "The truth is, yes."
>
> She said, "Don't you think that what we're doing is very hypocritical? We didn't go to Julia's wedding. We punish her without knowing if she deserves it or doesn't deserve it, and now we go to the burial with pomp and circumstance as if we were innocent."
>
> "I think that you're looking at it from a very mistaken point of view," I said. "Brothers and sisters move apart and they get back together if they're made of the right stuff."
>
> "If Julia and I couldn't get back together, it was the dictatorship that killed her which is guilty. I'm not guilty."

VOICE 4

Uki Goñi

Finance and economics editor at the English-language daily Buenos Aires Herald; *political editor during the military dictatorship.*

There were disappearances going on every day, and many of them were journalists, as you probably know. At first nobody knew what was going on after the coup, which I think was pretty much welcomed by everybody at the time, because it put an end to a very violent situation that existed under Isabelita Perón. When people started disappearing, nobody really knew what was going on. But the fact remains that none of the Argentine press carried any of the stories. The way we found out about it, the *Herald* I mean, is that the *Herald* was run by a man called Robert Cox, who was editor at that time. So he was carrying these stories that he personally knew about, but what we didn't know was the extent to which it was happening at that time.

And I remember one day, just like the secretary who just now told me that there's someone to see me, she said there's a woman here who wants to speak to a journalist. Then they said why don't you talk to this woman. I think it was a woman on her own, and she said I've come to see you about my son who was kidnapped. And so we carried a little story on this. And the next day we had two mothers, and the next day we had four, and you know, within a week we had something like twenty mothers out there a day, telling us about their particular cases.

There had been violence all along, you know. In the early seventies, late sixties, there had been violence and kidnapping. Only that people who were being kidnapped before were businessmen or government officials, kidnapped by terrorist groups. There were disappearances or murders, or maybe just fifteen bodies would be found lying next to the highway somewhere. Mothers would say, "They've come and taken my son away, and I don't know why." At first, I supposed, nobody knew whether it was just a continuation of the other violence. It took a while before we realized that this was a new form of violence. You know, Bob Cox was our editor, and he said let's run these stories. We felt apprehensive, of course, but we had the support of our editor. After about a week of this, we started asking the women why they were coming to the *Herald*. We're just a small newspaper in a foreign language, a community newspaper. They said they'd been to all the newspapers, and nobody would talk to them. They were just stopped at the door.

In a situation like that there's no need for them, I suppose, to order the press to be silent. It's enough for them to know that it's best not to carry the stories, because you just kidnap a couple of journalists and the message gets across pretty fast. So I think it was out of fear that everybody decided to turn a blind eye. The fear was generalized throughout society. It wasn't just the press. Even over dinner, nobody would talk about disappearances because it was just too scary.

They would just say there were abductions, you know, they were taken away by people who seemed to be from the security forces. I remember at one stage when we started getting so many reports coming in, Bob Cox decided that we should set up some kind of policy to handle this. And we decided that we would not publish the story of any disappearance that wasn't substantiated by a charge at a police station. We told the mothers we'll publish your story, but instead of publishing just the news from that, we'll publish that at such and such a police station charges were made that somebody, so and so, was kidnapped. And the mothers, of course, got very upset, saying, "It's the police who took them away."

You know, Bob Cox did get arrested once for publishing an article. The government, at first, did issue a ban on the reporting of any terrorist activities. What Cox published was a meeting of some terrorist heads, chiefs, and I think it was not even in Argentina. And this was carried in the newspaper, and he was arrested because that was a terrorist activity. And he was held for one day, and we eventually managed to get him out. So yes, there were intimidations and threats going on. I remember that Cox was often called in by various generals and admirals.

The *Herald*'s readers? I think we had lots of silent support. And I came across so many people. You'd meet mechanics somewhere—we had to translate the editorials, it comes out in English and Spanish—and they'd have the Spanish bit up on the wall. And so they bought the newspaper, even though they couldn't read English, just because they knew that the *Herald* had this particular stance on the issue. Many of the *Herald*'s sort of pro-readers, like the British community, were very conservative, were very upset about the *Herald*'s position. But I think the general reactions were apathy, or they just preferred to ignore it. I think that people who are *Herald* readers (and being somebody who worked there at the time, you know, I'd meet them socially, and this issue would just be ignored), they'd talk about "The Wizard of Id" or whatever else we carried because, as I said, people didn't talk about disappearances.

When the military eventually left and we had a trial against the members of the Junta, lots of people would suddenly say, "*Yo no sabía*"

("I didn't know"), and of course it's very hard to believe that. So the pretense carried on even as far as saying that they didn't know years later. At the time, most people turned a blind eye to it, and then, afterward, when it was obvious and it couldn't be ignored, people pretended that they didn't know in the first place.

I think that there's general apathy toward the subject. Argentina's a very conservative society. I think in their heart of hearts maybe many people agree that these people should have just been taken away. At the time, of course, we felt that if everybody published everything they knew, then it would stop. That would be the only way it would stop. But of course this did not occur. So are they guilty of omission? I think they definitely are guilty of omission. Who's going to judge this guilt? Because they were also afraid. The *Herald*, for some reason, managed to get away with it without too much damage. We lost our editor. But, of course, the other newspapers actually had journalists who were kidnapped and never seen again. So it's very difficult to answer. It was like a conspiracy of silence. It was definitely a conspiracy of silence. Whether it was a conspiracy of fear, or a conspiracy of supporting the Dirty War, I don't know. Probably a conspiracy of fear. The *Herald* was everybody's conscience, you know, Argentina's conscience speaking at the time. That's what it was, and that's why nobody wanted to hear it.

V

The Clinic

The Nuestra Señora de Luján Clinic on 643 Las Malvinas Street, is a
noisy, busy place, situated in the middle of Lomas de Zamora, a sub-
urb of dusty streets and crumbling sidewalks, half an hour by train
outside of Buenos Aires. Worried-looking patients fill the rows of bol-
ted-down plastic chairs, nursing their broken arms or applying direct
pressure with rags to their cuts. Some stand, making room for others
holding screaming babies. Workmen push trolleys past them, heavily
laden with potatoes and carrots destined for the kitchen, through the
waiting room and down a long hall. Doors swing open and closed.
There is a line to see the receptionist. A pregnant woman doesn't
know what form to fill out, and she starts to cry. Once in a while, a
man in a white smock rushes by.

The clinic hasn't changed much since Julia worked there in 1977.
Its patients are mostly the same as they have always been, blue-collar

workers, mestizos from the poorer barrios. The doctors there as well are still much the same, harassed, tired, with dark rings under their eyes.

Every Thursday Julia commuted to Lomas de Zamora from her home in Buenos Aires to work the night shift at the clinic. The job in Lomas was going to be only temporary, she had told her friends. As soon as her husband graduated, they would go south and start a new life together.

Julia was unable to complete these plans, however, because at about nine o'clock, March 6, 1977, a group of heavily armed men burst into the clinic, identifying themselves as members of the "security forces." They put a hood over Julia's head and began to drag her, kicking and screaming, out of the clinic. The son of one of the directors of the clinic who lived next door heard what was going on and attempted to intervene. He was severely beaten by the armed group and was unable to stop Julia from being taken away in one of the two waiting cars.

This version of Julia's kidnapping was repeated frequently in testimony by Julia's friends and family. It cannot, however, be confirmed. Without a doubt, the agents of the military government were responsible for Julia's kidnapping because she was soon sighted (according to eyewitness accounts) at various clandestine prison camps under their control. Nevertheless, no one knows from what source this story of the kidnapping originated or what part or parts of it are true.

In the hopes of interviewing someone who had witnessed Julia's disappearance, I traveled to the clinic. Waiting among the patients in the waiting room, I finally made contact with a secretary named Norma. With a smile and an apologetic face, Norma explained that she herself had not been working at the clinic at the time of Julia's kidnapping, but she confirmed the story of what had happened, saying that she had learned about it from doctors who had once worked there. She wanted to be helpful, but as far as she knew, no one from that time still worked at Nuestra Señora de Luján. After all, she said, it was a long time ago, and clinics go through many changes.

Norma then introduced me to Dr. Russo, head of the clinic archives. He expressed ignorance about the kidnapping, but, like

Norma, he assured me that if there was any information in the archives, he would be happy to provide it. Norma added that she could also give out the names and addresses of the ex-directors of the clinic, anything, really, that could be helpful. "Come back next week," she said.

The next time I returned to Nuestra Señora de Luján, there was going to be a strike by the clinic employees. It was a bad time for her, Norma said. "Couldn't you come back next week?" The next day when I returned, Norma was out to lunch. The next, she had to go to the bank. The next, she was nowhere to be found. And as for Dr. Russo, I began to spend more and more hours in the waiting room each successive afternoon until I was told by the receptionist that the doctor had left for the day. No, she couldn't say when he would return.

Several weeks afterwards, I saw Norma again. As Dr. Russo was still nowhere to be found, Norma reluctantly agreed to introduce me to the second-in-charge of archives. The first remarks this elderly woman doctor uttered upon being asked about Julia was, "She was an extremist, wasn't she? All of the people who were taken away were extremists." She was well aware of this, she went on to say, because she had had a cousin who had been an extremist, and she had been made to disappear. However, neither the archivist nor the rest of her family had been bothered by the military, an obvious sign that they took away only people who had done something to deserve it.

Furthermore, the clinic's records would be in no way useful. No one had ever recorded Julia's disappearance. (Archives just weren't meant for that sort of information, she said.) Anyway, she even doubted that Julia had been kidnapped. According to what she had heard, Julia had hidden in a bathroom when the military group came in, and she had managed to escape. As for the name of anyone who had worked on the night shift with Julia or the names of the ex-directors of the hospital, releasing this information was not allowed and would require the authorization of the current directors as well as an "official" letter stating why anyone would want such information. She stood up and said that she was sorry she couldn't help anymore, but she had things to do. As she ushered me out the door, she asked, "What year did you say this woman was taken away?"

Farther down the hallway, I ran into Norma again and asked whether it was possible to interview the ex-directors as we had discussed before. Norma responded, "I wasn't here. I don't want to get involved anymore," and hurried off down the hallway. I never saw her again.

All my attempts to interview the current directors proved fruitless. I telephoned on several occasions and was told that the directors had either just left the clinic, or they had just shown up and were busy working, or they had just gone on vacation and couldn't be reached, or they had just returned and were too tired to give interviews. Call again next Wednesday, next Monday, next Tuesday. As I continued to call, and the days turned into weeks and the weeks months, it was obvious that March 6, 1977, was a day lost to history.

In its 1984 investigation of Julia's disappearance, the National Commission on the Disappearance of People (CONADEP), a non-government group convened to investigate the horrors of the Dirty War, contacted the former directors of the clinic and asked them to present testimony on the matter. According to the files at CONADEP, none of them ever did. In 1991, the anthropologists who had discovered Julia's remains informed the clinic of their findings. No one from the clinic attended Julia's funeral, nor was there ever an official reply. They were well within their rights not to give testimony, as CONADEP was an organization independent of the Argentine government and did not have the power of subpoena. As for the funeral, it had been merely a personal request.

Life upon life of family members and friends was shattered the day Julia Andrea disappeared, and yet it is these people who gather enough courage to talk about what happened to them. Ex-prisoners and political militants, those who repeated time and time again to me, "Don't use my real name, because I'm afraid they'll find me," those who have the most to lose if the military again returns to power, talk. They talk through their fear and through their pain because they cannot stand the silence. It is the opinion of many of them that the action of the clinic personnel implies that they were accomplices, that they had a hand in Julia's kidnapping, or that they at least played a part in covering up her disappearance. Why else, they ask, would the doctors remain silent for so many years?

The answer, most probably, is not as sinister as those surviving Julia tend to believe. The clinic personnel are neither pro-dictatorship nor pro–human rights. They are only, and quite blithely, pro-themselves. They are an example of the silent Argentines, those who were not among the masses that filled the Plaza de Mayo to laud the military's efforts during the Malvinas War, those who did not fill the plaza to demand a return to democracy. They did not fire the shot that killed Julia. They did not steal her child. But neither did they protest the death of thousands while the mass murders were going on, nor do they show an interest today in knowing the fate of the many missing children, such as Julia's, who still lie hidden under false names, who live in false families. They are the ones who made the phrase *No te metas* ("Don't get involved") famous.

The personnel at la Clínica Nuestra Señora de Luján come neither to praise nor to bury Caesar. They wait and see what happens to him. They wait and see and watch and allow to go by unchecked all the atrocities committed during the Dirty War because "It didn't happen to my family," says the second-in-charge of archives, because "I don't want to get involved," says Norma, because Dr. Russo and the directors of the clinic said and still continue to say nothing at all.

As one walks down the corridor of la Clínica Nuestra Señora de Luján, down the small ramp and into the hot Argentine night for the train ride back to Buenos Aires, one is almost convinced that the last sound one hears, among the noise and the confusion, is that of faint applause.

VOICE 5

María Adela Gard de Antokoletz

Representative of the Madres de la Plaza de Mayo, Linea
Fundadora (Mothers of the Plaza de Mayo); human
rights lecturer and activist.

A few years ago, two years, almost three, when we were protesting against the presidential pardon of war criminals, two men passed me in the street, stopped, and came back (the men were about forty or forty-five years old) and said, "Señora, we're not going to sign. We think about you, we're horrified by what happened, we don't want, like you say, for this to happen ever again. But we're afraid that they'll kill us, we're afraid of losing our jobs, we're afraid of repression. Afraid, in a word, of anything. Forgive us, but we're not going to sign."

There is no security. If the government of ex-President Alfonsín and the government of current President Menem had satisfied our request to clarify what went on, we could have had justice and punishment for the guilty. As long as this doesn't happen, there's always going to be fear of the police, with their itchy trigger fingers, who know nothing ever happens to them. All of this makes you live in insecurity. There is fear in the country.

We say "thirty thousand *desaparecidos*" but these are the determinations of the human rights organizations. In Jujuy there's a mine that has been extremely rich in silver. In this mine ninety people disappeared—there's only one official complaint. Only one. Here, going from Buenos Aires to Rosario, there's a large factory called Talmed. In Talmed there disappeared and were killed (the number goes for both) two hundred fifty people. There are seventy official complaints. Of the disappeared who were from a military family, the families didn't lodge a complaint, except in rare cases.

The soldier here has always been considered something apart from society, on a higher level, and because his son, his daughter, his close relative, was associated with those they called *la subversión*, he would take it as an affront, as a shame, as something completely painful and negative for the family. Because of this, he didn't say anything. Clearly, on one side there was the person who wanted justice, liberty, equality, the same opportunities for everyone, war against poverty. On the other side, there's the person who was repressing all of this. It's a very difficult situation, very difficult. Therefore be quiet. Be quiet.

A lot of this shameful behavior comes from the Catholic Church. In every situation where men are involved, there are always exceptions, right? But among the eighty-three bishops who were there at this time, five or six of them were there with the gospel in hand, at the side of the poorest, of those who were the most needy, who were ourselves: the mothers of the disappeared, the sisters, the daughters, the grandchildren, the wives, the husbands. In reality, the Church denied us. We didn't have a Church, because its upper hierarchy betrayed us. If the Church had intervened like the power it was, the power that it continues to be, it could have saved a lot of people.

The disappeared person is attacked because he's capable, because he has ideas, because he teaches responsibilities to the rest. Therefore, he's a danger, a clear danger to the system. Then, what is the method that doesn't hurt the state, the government? Make the person disappear, without a high political cost. It was as if they were packages. Make the person disappear without leaving signs, as if they hadn't been born, or hadn't gone to school, or hadn't lived. It is to erase from society a disturbing part for the sake of those who don't want things to change, because if things change, they're not going to be in power. That's how I understand disappearance.

Why did they take away my son? He didn't belong to any political organization. (I'm not saying this in order to make excuses. It was only right that they belonged to the organizations that they belonged to.) But he didn't belong to any organization. He wasn't interested in politics at all. But I want to say that he was a lawyer, a legal investigator, with a specialization in international public law. He was making his name already. He had been invited to all the legal conventions inside and outside the country. He couldn't go, however, because he was poor. He didn't have a car. He didn't have his own apartment. He couldn't go to the events in Europe.

At this time, when they began to make people disappear and lock them up, the families of these people asked my son to work with political prisoners. And he accepted. And because of the way he was, he didn't charge them anything for his work, because he considered that these people were oppressed by a situation many times unjust. He charged only for expenses because he was a poor lawyer. He had a prisoner in Resistencia, there, far in the north. He was going to Resistencia, and they had moved the prisoner to Rawson and hadn't told him about it. He didn't give up though, and he continued to help the man. You could say that my son established his legal office in the hallways of the tribunals. Every day he went to the tribunals, and he didn't eat much. Every day. They had to make him disappear.

There are a lot of cases like his, of girls who taught women in the slums how to cook. It might seem like a lie, but poor people are ignorant in every sense. They don't know how to handle themselves. They don't know how to survive with the very few pesos that they have. They don't know how to cook well and cheap. They don't know how to bathe a child. They don't know anything. You've got to teach them everything.

They found it extremely dangerous. The girls of the mothers who marched with me, many of them were girls who went to the slums to teach children how to write who had never learned in a school, or to raise a few pesos to establish a clinic and to bring medication.

I was in Germany (I can't say the exact year), but it was when Germany was observing its fortieth anniversary after all the atrocities that had been committed there, and there were debates whether they should continue with actions against those people who committed atrocities. And the same day the representatives decided to continue pursuing authors of war crimes. As if in forty years there was the complete assurance that many of them were still left.

A society that does not fight for its rights becomes a sick society, a society that lives in fear and horror that it can happen again. That is what happens here in Argentina, and this is what makes us, the human rights organizations, survive. We can't sit peacefully at home. I'm really old. I'm eighty-one years old. I shouldn't go outside in this heat. I shouldn't. It's something that goes against me, but I can't stay at home. I have vowed that I will come Mondays and Wednesdays to the Mothers' office, and I'm going to keep on coming, Mondays and Wednesdays, as long as I have the strength to do so. That's why I tell you, it's the least I can do for my son and the other disappeared people, so that this doesn't happen again, so that no one disappears again, not here or anywhere else. Because if we hadn't gone outside, if we had stayed quiet, if there weren't groups that keep track of the numbers of disappeared, there would still have been disappearances, and we would continue to have disappearances.

The mothers who didn't fight, who are ten and fifteen years younger than I, look like sick, old women. They are destroyed. Completely destroyed. When we go to the plaza on Thursdays, some mothers say to me, "How few, María Adela, how few of us have come, how few of us there are!" I believe that we're really not few because we were a group that marched. Although there are spaces in this wheel, for sixteen years now we go every Thursday to the plaza. It's clear proof that things are bad and that they need solutions.

There are many young people who want to know and who condemn what has gone on. In terms of the society, I say there is a division, the people who are fifty years old and above, and those below. The younger people listen. They want to know, and they ask questions. The others don't.

V I

Laura

During the last few years of medical school, the Montesini family began to have financial problems. This forced Julia to work at several jobs to pay for her studies. Her first job, taken out of necessity, was as an administrator for a company that distributed cheese and pork products. Her second job, as night guard at a home for mentally handicapped girls, had much more to do with pediatrics, the specialization in medicine to which she aspired.

Laura had already been working at the home for several years when Julia began working there; it was Laura's job to introduce Julia around and explain to her what her duties would be. Laura says that after having worked for twenty-four years with physically and mentally handicapped children, she made friends with only two coworkers. Julia was one of them. Laura recalls Julia's first day of work:

When a new person comes to work, it's normal to have nothing to do with them, right? When new people came in, I taught them how to do what I had learned, and what's more, not to be afraid, because you had these girls, and some were pretty deformed. So I said, "Look, you don't have to be afraid. With these girls you work like this"—you take them to their bedrooms, to the toilets, to the showers . . . the schedules that we had to give them their medicine. At night, we were alone. Therefore, you had to have courage when a girl was having a convulsion, give her the medicine that she had to take, and take her to the hospital. And so I was showing her what to do. We were walking throughout the entire institute, but my other work companion stayed where she was. She didn't take to Julia like I took to Julia and she to me. Well, I laughed later on because a few hours after she started work, she said to me, "It seems like we've known each other for years, because you have a really nice personality, you show a lot of solidarity, a real friend." Well, I am that way, and she was the same.

The work at the children's home was difficult, especially when the girls had seizures, or when they wouldn't take their medicine and settle down for the night. The struggle cost the women a lot, but the friendship formed that first night held, and Laura and Julia became inseparable at the institute. A strong relationship developed between the two women and with the children as well. When Laura and Julia arrived at night, some of the girls who could walk would come to them, put their arms around them, and kiss them. Sometimes it seemed hopeless, pitiful, working with the children, Laura explains, but it was this love that the children gave and received that saw Laura and Julia through. And some nights, as Laura remembers, they

> felt really content, because sometimes we actually taught one of the girls to eat—with her hand all twisted from a deformity, the only way she could—but when she ate, when she learned to eat, we were filled with joy. "We've done something great. We've won!"

When the children had been given their medicine and put to bed, Julia and Laura stayed up, drinking coffee and smoking cigarettes until morning. They gossiped, told each other intimate secrets, things they would never tell anyone else, but they never repeated what they had heard. They talked about everything, about films they had seen or wanted to see, about clothes and fashion. According to Laura, Julia dressed simply, "very humanly," and sometimes Laura sewed a bit of clothing for Julia. Above all, Julia talked about "the future, about graduating, being a doctor, dedicating herself to medicine—she was filled with it, because it fascinated her—getting married. Having kids. She wanted to have a lot of kids."

Julia could have chosen a different line of work, Laura supposes. She didn't need to have worked long nights, catching a few hours when everything was quiet to study for medical school the next day. She could have chosen an easier job, one that didn't mean such a commitment and that would have paid more. But then it wouldn't have been Julia. She had to put herself into what she did, she had to be herself, or she couldn't do it. Laura says:

> I think Julia chose this work because she really liked to help peo-
> ple. Moreover, she dedicated herself to the children. Look, after
> all those days and months and years, it was really easy for her to
> work with the girls—to see her working!—because when a person
> dedicates herself with love and when a person works because she
> cares for . . . the children . . . it's a wonderful thing. I think it was
> because of this that I got along so well with Julia, because we
> were very similar in this sense. We worked giving love to the
> girls, although they didn't understand. I really felt good, Julia as
> well, because that's why we were there, to help the people. All in
> all, the people like us who thought this way suffered the most,
> no? The people who didn't care much about anything suffered
> less. Well, I feel okay the way I am, and Julia too.

When Laura first met Julia, Laura was going through a difficult time in her life; she needed help, and she turned to Julia. She was thinking of getting divorced from her alcoholic and abusive husband,

and she was especially worried about her young daughter. She didn't think that it was good for the child to see her father acting in such a way, but she didn't know what kind of effect a divorce would have on her. Julia counseled Laura, helped her not to feel badly about wanting a divorce, told her that she had to think of her child. When Laura finally decided to seek the divorce, Julia accompanied her to the lawyer's office, convincing her that it was the right decision to make. During the interim, Julia invited Laura to her house to meet her parents and to spend a few days there with her child. Laura says:

> I was always very strong, but there comes a time when you have to think about getting divorced, and, well, I felt that Julia was really there for me. When you're going through a rough moment, the most important thing, let's say, is to have some spiritual support, someone to listen to you, someone to talk to you, to raise your spirits a little.

At the time when Laura's relationship with Julia and the Montesini family was growing stronger, the political condition in Argentina was rapidly deteriorating. Laura remembers walking to the children's home at night, afraid of snipers and the rainbow array of paramilitary groups, soldiers, and police. Although she was afraid, she carried with her that imaginary talisman of protection that many Argentines had: her lack of political involvement. She thought that if she wasn't doing anything wrong, she would be left unharmed, a fatal misjudgment common to many of the soon-to-be-disappeared. Laura was, in fact, antipolitical, as much in her distaste for politicians as in her social pessimism. For quite a long time Laura had no idea which way the political tides were moving, but as she slowly began to understand the political movements and the armed struggle, she "always thought it was useless, that nothing was ever going to be fixed. Just the opposite. Things got worse."

After the ransacking of the Montesini house on May 13, 1975, Julia's family decided it was too dangerous to stay in Pilar de la Sierra. After they left their house, Laura remembers that Julia was afraid to go back even to collect her clothes, so Laura went for them. Laura knew that this act, no matter how insignificant, compromised her and that the people who kept watch on the Montesini house would take her for a militant. Laura maintains, however, that what she did was a purely apolitical act:

> I helped her because—I'll repeat myself—Julia was my friend, her family were friends of mine. They helped me in my moment of need. I'm a grateful person, and if you're my friend, you're my friend through good times and bad. I don't have problems with helping people. I did it with my whole heart. I had problems because people distanced themselves from me, thinking that I, too, was a militant. I never "militated" in anything. And if I had, I would tell you. But I didn't. I believed in the justice from up above, of God, not in the justice of man. Then God knows that I didn't do anything, simply helping the people that I loved. I always thought that it was all in vain, because when you have good intentions, that's when you're the most persecuted.

Laura insists that she was never afraid of being taken away, an assertion that she had a chance to prove a few weeks after Julia had been disappeared. Two police cars stopped in front of her house, and she thought, well, it's finally come, they're going to talk to me. She waited for the knock on the door. Hours passed and nothing. She looked through the window. One car left and was replaced by another. Tired of waiting, Laura did what in retrospect seems absurd; she went outside and waited on the front sidewalk so that the police could see she was there and get on with it.

Fortunately for Laura, the police were actually laying a trap for someone a few blocks down the street from her house. She was never harassed in any way, and the knock that she had expected for so many years never came.

Laura's mixture of innocence and ingenuity may or may not have been the factor that saved her from being taken. The thousands of testimonies collected by the National Commission on the Disappearance of People, as well as by other human rights agencies, show that innocence was not taken into account by the military machine, and that often if a mistake was made and the wrong person kidnapped, then he or she was a liability to be disposed of.

Why was Julia taken? This is a question Laura has often asked herself. It was obvious that Julia loved her brother, Luis Ignacio, very much. She would follow him from place to place. Julia would say that she was meeting her brother, but she wouldn't say when or where, nor would she tell Laura what they talked about. Laura remembers Julia once saying, "Don't get involved. I don't want you to know, because if something happens to you, which I hope never does, and if you say, 'Yes, yes, such and such,' then they're going to think that you're a militant, too."

Laura maintains that she didn't know whether Julia was an activist, an armed militant, or if she just followed Luis Ignacio around because of the love and respect that she had for him. For one of these reasons, perhaps all of them, Laura thinks, Julia was murdered. Laura argued on several occasions with Julia, trying to convince her that whatever she was doing was better left undone, that it wouldn't make a difference anyway, that nothing was every going to change. She should take advantage of her education, set up her practice, help the people that she had been trained to help. Julia replied that she would remain true to her ideals, that she wouldn't change. She was going to make a difference in spite of everything.

From 1977 until the arrival of democracy in 1983, Laura says she was never afraid to talk about Julia, but she admitted to me that

> after all these years, I'll tell you honestly, when I learned that you wanted to talk to me, after all these years (I'm a lot older, aren't I?) I felt a little afraid. Because of this, I thought, "I don't know if I'm going to talk," because now, after seeing it all, after seeing how it all turned out, that I lost people, Julia, Luis Ignacio, really good people, that they disappeared, now I feel a little bit afraid. Look how many years ago this was! Now I feel afraid. I don't want anything to happen to me. My daughter is married. I want, I want peace. I want tranquillity, which is difficult.

Laura's search for peace did not allow her to go to Julia's funeral. She couldn't go, she says. She couldn't bear to stand in front of the crypt, in front of a small box that contained what was left of Julia, her work companion, her night-long talker, bather of children, friend, counselor:

> Julia, I remember the last time I saw her, and, for me, she still remains alive. I'm going to remember her like that. The last time she was at home and said "Well, I've got to go to work," and, I remember that we said good-bye, "Ciao, see you soon, we'll be seeing each other." But I never saw her again. It's like I wait for her, and she's going to return.

VOICE 6

Adolfo Pérez Esquivel

*Recipient of the 1980 Nobel Peace Prize; representative of
the international human rights organization Servicio de
Paz y Justicia (SERPAJ—Service for Peace and Justice).*

A great violence began to occur in this country, 1974, 1975: kidnappings, torture, disappearances. And we at what was to become SERPAJ began to work with Chilean refugees after Pinochet's military coup in Chile. We coordinated with churches in other countries (as was the case with Canada) trying to make it possible for these people to leave for a third country, where they would be given a visa and possibilities for life and work. And, also, there were the most immediate necessities of the families which were affected. We also began to work on complaints concerning the situation, and we published a book called *Human Rights and the Latin American Reality*, which was nothing more than a reflection of the Universal Declaration of Human Rights, declarations at the ecumenical level of the churches, and references concerning the situation in certain Latin American countries. Logically, there were things concerning Argentina, Brazil, all countries. This really bothered the military here, so much so that they threatened the print shop, which was associated with a religious school. They began to watch our headquarters. There were threats as well.

When the military coup occurred March 24, 1976, I had already scheduled since the year before a trip through Europe. Five days after the coup, I left the country, although I had to pass through six military checkpoints and two checks in the airplane as I was seated in the plane. But I left the country and began to travel through Europe. When I was in Bern, Switzerland, I received an urgent call from Austria, telling me that our SERPAJ headquarters in Argentina had been surrounded by the police and that all of my coworkers, including my son, were taken prisoner. That was when we started a very intense international campaign in order to have my son released.

My wife had traveled to Europe also and we had two small children who were being taken care of by my sister-in-law, but we had to place them under the protection of an embassy, and the embassy went to look for them, and they took all my family to the embassy, including the oldest, once he was freed. I'm not going to say the name of the embassy for obvious reasons. You've got to be careful with these things. After many difficulties with the military government, the release of my children was achieved, all of them minors. One of them, the youngest, was five years old . . . very "subversive."

Well, we were able to get them out of the country. They went to Switzerland, we got together there, and afterwards we went to France. Afterwards, we decided to go to Ecuador because our work needed to continue within Latin America. In Ecuador an event occurred, because the persecution wasn't only in Argentina, it was also going on in many other countries. In Ecuador, there was a meeting of Latin American bishops, at which the bishops asked that I go in an advisory capacity to Riobamba, Ecuador. And among these Latin American bishops there were four bishops from the United States who didn't believe us when we told them what was going on in Latin America. That is, until they found a machine gun pointed at their stomachs. Because this meeting of priests, of theologians, of Christians, was repressed by a battalion of more than seventy soldiers. All of us spent some time in jail in Ecuador.

They deported a first group, they deported me, and my oldest son. They didn't touch my younger children or my wife. They deported us to Colombia. We decided to return to Argentina.

Although we knew that there was danger, we thought, well, nothing was going to happen. Anyway, we had placed an international advisory [memo] as a precaution. We didn't have any problems. We returned easily, nothing happened. We went home. And I had to renew my passport, and I went to the police department to do this. I finished the renewal of the passport. Fifteen days later I went to pick it up, and when I went to pick it up, that was April 4, 1977, they took me prisoner. This meant a lot to me because April 4 is the anniversary of the assassination of Martin Luther King. And it was the first day in Easter holy week.

They took me to the Superintendencia de Seguridad Federal, a torture center, at which there weren't a lot of people at that moment. The people had been taken out already, but the traces were left in this torture center of the Federal Police, at Moreno Street, 1547, one block from the police department. There were striking things there. I was locked up in a *tubo*. A *tubo* is a small cell, like this table. It was more or less one meter wide by two meters or one meter, eighty [centimeters], nothing more. I was there for thirty-two days.

There was a small mattress filled with urine. There was a nauseating smell. It was all dark. There was only a small peephole, really small, through which the guards shone a lantern to see if I was there or if I had escaped. This was a torture center, tremendous, because I remember that when that guard opened the door, because I had to knock on the door in order to go the bathroom, or I had to do it there. And there wasn't anything there. Because of this there was such a terrible smell.

They would open the door and the light from the corridor would enter, in a space there. I could see the wall filled with inscriptions, slogans, names of soccer clubs, insults, prayers, names of loved ones, but what remained with me, forever recorded, was a large blood stain (the rope and blindfolds that they put on the prisoners were still thrown on the floor), a large blood stain on the wall, and someone wrote with his finger tip, in blood, "God doesn't kill." There were insults for the police, there was also a star of David. There were Christian crosses. It was the history of the victims of all this madness.

My wife kept insisting to see me, and they denied that I was there. If she hadn't done that, I would have been one *desaparecido* more. But my wife insisted that they had detained me at the police department, when she was present. The first organization that protested to the Argentine government was the Episcopal Conference of the United States. (Afterwards, Kennedy and, well, a lot of senators mobilized support for the disappeared, and there were a lot of protests on the international level.) A guard came and said to me, "You're the one that the yankee bishops are defending? Because they just told us that the Episcopal Conference of the United States is asking for you." Incredible. But it was that way.

My wife succeeded in seeing me after three days, and then they took me to a corridor with bars: the *leoneras* (lion cages) were large cells, one for men and another for women. They're called that in prison slang. One of the things that really shocked me was—am I in Argentina or in Nazi Germany, no?—painted on a large wall, almost covering the wall was the swastika, and written below it was Nationalism, spelled with a z. And there were also a lot of little swastikas painted on the walls by the guards, with mottoes like "Leftist, we're gonna get you!" "Commander Good-Time," "Commander Tiger." This large swastika was a symbol of all this, of what was there, because it was painted with the ink roller with which they took our finger prints, and they did it with that.

One day, early in the morning, they took me out. This was May 5, 1977. They took me to the airport in San Justo. In the province of Buenos Aires, there is a hanger that is, on one side, a sport club, and on the other side, part of the police. So they took me to a little airplane. I don't know why, because it was a trip from Buenos Aires to La Plata, some sixty kilometers. At this hour, it was three or four in the morning. We could get there in, I don't know, thirty or forty minutes. But they took me out, and they had me flying about two hours.

They were going to throw me in the river, or in the sea, like they threw so many prisoners whose bodies appeared later off the coast of Uruguay. So I was coming in the airplane, and it was turning, turning, turning. We were going all over the place, but we weren't landing. It was like an hour, an hour and a half, a long time, until the plane landed at the air base in Morrón, at the military base. At this base, they didn't let me get out of the airplane; I remained in chains.

I'm there waiting and they told me that it's to refuel the airplane, and then one hour, one and a half hours, two hours, and later they came back and told me, "Relax, we're going to take you to the Unidad Nueve prison in La Plata." At this moment they were discussing if I should remain alive or not, if they were going to kill me, if they were going to throw me out of the airplane, if they were going to liquidate me. And when they told me they were going to take me to the Unidad Nueve, well, I breathed a bit easier. They took me to the Unidad Nueve in La Plata. I was there for fourteen months.

I was tortured there for five days. It was the punishment cell, the cell that's called *la chanchera*, the pigsty, that's where they brought the people who were punished, where they tortured you. I was there until the international campaign succeeded in freeing me, one day before the final match of the World Soccer Championship, with Holland against Argentina. This day, the world final, because of the struggle, the international struggle, to relax the international tensions, they freed me, but it was "freedom under surveillance." The entire process with me was nothing normal because the man who took me out of jail in chains was one of the most terrible murderers who is presently free, who at that time was called Major Guastavino, and whose real name is Guglielminetti, one of the repressors, who always went about dressed in his uniform in the prison.

He took prisoners away, and these prisoners disappeared. This man

looked for me in the cell, he put me in a Ford Falcon, and he took me
to the Primer Puerto of the Army in Palermo, at this time under the
command of General Suárez Mason, as commander of the first army
corps, which was the center of repressive operations. And this Guglielminetti, who was called Major Gustavino, his *nombre de guerra*, says
"I'm going to take you to your house, and you're free but under obser-
vation." That is to say, I could move in only a very small circle, and I
was controlled by the police, the military, and I had to present myself
twice weekly at the police station. And if I disobeyed this I could be
sentenced to eight years in prison.

Several countries had offered me the right to asylum, to leave the
country. I didn't want to leave the country. I preferred to stay in the
country. I thought that it was the moment to stay and not to subject
my family to what they had gone through before. So I stayed there in
my house under police and military pressure.

Well, I was there for fourteen months, one of the longest "freedoms
under surveillance" in the country. And, it was recently in 1979, in
June 1979, that they granted me complete freedom. But during all this
time I was in prison, two women from Northern Ireland, recipients
themselves of the Nobel, proposed me as a candidate for the Nobel
Peace Prize. And there began the campaign for the Nobel. And other
international recognition had also arrived at this time. Well, they
awarded me the prize in 1980.

We had two assassination attempts. One was when I was with my
son, when we arrived at the headquarters of SERPAJ, and two people
appeared with guns to kill us and a taxi crossed in front of us, and we
escaped. But if it hadn't been for the taxi, they would have killed us.
And another was when Joan Baez came to visit us. She was with us.
They wouldn't let her sing. They followed her in the hotels where she
was just because she came to visit me.

And when she came to the headquarters, they placed a trotil bomb
with more than two kilos of trotil in the window of our building, in
the old building, which is in 479 México Street. There, in the window,
they put a packet of trotil, and, luckily, a workmate of mine realized
this and told us, and we took Joan Baez and all the people in the

building, we took her, running out of the building in order to get as far away as possible. We called the bomb squad to find out what this was all about. The bomb squad deactivated the bomb, but it was meant to blow up the entire block. So, poor Joan Baez had a very bad time here.

In the final analysis, there are other people who aren't able to talk about these things. Other people have been through a lot more terrible things than I have. When I talk, I always think that I had international support. I had people who looked after me. I knew that there were people in the world, in all the countries, who were running campaigns, who were protesting in front of embassies, who were sending letters, who held demonstrations. That is to say, I wasn't without protection. Is that clear?

But I think about all my friends in the prison, many of whom ended up crazy or destroyed—completely destroyed—who didn't have anyone, not even a family that went to visit them, because of fear, because the family had disintegrated. And they took many prisoners away from there, killed them, and what more we don't know up until this very day. I believe that in my case, well, my life was saved thanks to international solidarity. If it hadn't been for that, they would have killed me right away. And not because I was a guerrilla, not anything like that, but because I worked for peace, for human rights, not with violence. Because all of our politics has to do with nonviolence, all of what we do, all of our work, within the Christian movements. And I always think about these people who didn't have anyone's help, who were really alone. I never felt alone, because eighty thousand things could happen to me, but I knew that people were helping me. But thousands of prisoners had no one.

V I I

Luciano

"Luciano is a changed man," his mother says, as she leads the way to his house, pausing for a moment to wipe the sweat from her forehead. Orange trees line the sidewalks of Villa María, and the sun bakes down on anyone in this small rural town who hasn't chosen wisely to stay inside for the siesta. "He used to be a genius, you know."

Although her son lives just a few blocks from her house, he doesn't come to visit her. He used to, she says, but that was years ago. Luciano Marquez was once a brilliant surgeon, a man who seemed capable of pulling his patients back from death as much through his force of will as through his uncanny medical ability. But that, too, was years ago. Luciano no longer practices medicine. After choosing retirement, or being forced to retire (which of the two is closer to the truth isn't quite clear) a few years ago, he now lives in the vast house that once served as his medical offices.

Luciano's mother doesn't know what changed him. She says perhaps it was the car accident a few years ago, when he received such a
severe blow to his head that he lay in intensive care for weeks and
almost did not recover. Perhaps it was the stress of knowing that the
woman passenger riding with him died. Or perhaps, going even further back, it was the pain and guilt Luciano felt after learning that his
former girlfriend, with whom he had ended on bad terms, had been
kidnapped and murdered. Whatever the cause, his mother says, Luciano is not the same man he used to be.

Luciano's house isn't visible from the street; it is concealed by a tall
wooden fence. "Don't worry," his mother says, as she rings the doorbell. "He'll answer your questions—especially about Julia."

Luciano responds through the intercom, a distant voice. After a
jangle of keys, he opens the door. He looks much the same as the
photographs his mother has of him from the 1960s, although his thin
face is more haggard now, and his long beard is graying instead of
black. He stands without a shirt, deep eyes gazing, several braided
bracelets hanging on his wrist. Mother and son argue at the gate. She
asks him to come visit some day. He sends her away, muttering something about overprotective parents.

He leads me through the open-air patio with its high walls, past the
many chambers where he used to practice medicine, and he unlocks
another set of doors. Just within the entrance of the kitchen, Luciano
is quick to point out a small bed pushed against the wall. No one is
allowed to sit on it, he says.

It is covered with assorted objects: a heavily underlined copy of
Nunca Más, its pages pressed down in sections; Luciano's old black
medical bag; a human skull from some anatomy class; a collection of
small boxes; a notebook filled with newspaper articles and photocopies
about Julia's burial. Luciano gets out a box of matches and lights the
gas stove. Pointing to the bed, he explains that when he and Julia used
to study medicine together in Córdoba, they spread their books and
notes over the thin mattress, lounged around her small apartment,
and drank mate, a strong Argentine tea. With these objects that have
to do with Julia, he has made the bed into a sort of museum, a memo-

rial. It is "Julia's bed," he says, and, because of this, no one is allowed to sit on it.

Luciano walks about the kitchen, a bit perplexed, drinking mate in the Argentine style from a gourd and a thick metal straw, and chain-smoking cigarettes. He taps the packet of cigarettes with his forefinger for a moment and admits, "My only bad habit." He pours more hot water for the mate and then sits down at the kitchen table, a concentrated look in his eyes. He met Julia in 1967, he explains, but they never had a specific day that they called their anniversary. They met in a class one day, at medical school, and what started out as a friendship turned into something more. He pauses for a moment, disturbed because he can't give a specific date for when he first met Julia. Chronological order is very important, he says, in trying to understand all that went on.

Luciano begins to explain how much he cared for Julia, but then he interrupts himself in mid-sentence to talk about the causes of political repression during the 1970s. Soon he is back discussing Julia and the way she was in the 1960s. Then, somewhere between the international soccer championship in 1978 and the end of the dictatorship in 1983, Luciano gets up from the kitchen table to see if the tea water is ready. As he pours hot water into the gourd, he persists in his monologue of assertions, retractions, and incomplete sentences. Punctuated by short pauses and laughter, inhaling cigarette smoke and drinking mate, the general meaning of what Luciano seems to want to say is gleaned, but much of the sense of it is lost.

Luciano stops talking for a moment and lights another cigarette. Having tried to form a sort of order from his thoughts and finding himself unable, he gets up from the table and walks to the bed set against the wall. Half-sitting on the bed, half-kneeling, he sorts through the objects spread across the mattress. They seem to reassure him, focus him, and it becomes apparent that these objects, more than Luciano's words, will tell his story for him.

Luciano pulls out a thin, silver medallion from a small cardboard box. He lifts it to show how it shines in the light and then puts it away again, folding the crease in the box lid carefully and laying it on the bed. It was a gift from Julia, he says, more precious than what it cost because she didn't have much money, but she bought the medallion for him anyway. Luciano now wears a wooden cross on a cord tied about his neck. He doesn't believe in God, he says, but he's accustomed to wearing the cord—having used it for a sling after his arm was damaged in the car crash—and a friend gave him the cross to put on it. He likes the way it looks, he says. No, he'd never be able to wear Julia's medallion; it's too precious.

He picks up a small, rectangular box, another present from Julia: a silver pen and pencil set. He used to use them, he says, but now, afraid of losing them, he keeps them safely on the bed.

Wandering in and out of time periods, Luciano says that one day when he was looking for a replacement cartridge for the pen, he took the backing off the box. It was there he found a small piece of paper that he'd never seen before. It said "I Love You," in English, a note from Julia that he still keeps neatly folded in the back of the box. He and Julia used to pass little notes as they studied together, or they whispered a few words in English so that the other study partners wouldn't understand. "It was our joke," Luciano explains. Now, years after her death, years after he stopped dating her, Julia is still there, telling Luciano that she loves him. That is how Julia seems to be in Luciano's house, always reappearing, always behind everything he sees.

All around the kitchen there are photographs of Julia with Luciano, or Julia alone, taped to the tiles, propped loosely along the shelves. Luciano points to a picture of Julia straddling a large blue buoy on a beach, smiling, arms held tight to the float like a cowboy bracing against a great bull. They had come across the buoy while on vacation at the seaside, and Luciano had urged Julia to climb on top so that he could take her picture. Afterwards, they decided that the buoy was out of place on land, stranded, so they tried to drag it back to the sea where it belonged, laughing and struggling for hours against its tremendous weight. Luciano doesn't make it clear whether they reached the water or not.

Luciano gets up to turn off the gas burner, remembering when they used to study in the library together, how Julia suddenly cleared the books away, got up on the table, and began a series of folk dances. "We would listen in total silence to the sound of her feet tapping," Luciano remembers with a smile. After she had finished dancing, the students cheered, Luciano helped her off the table, and they went back to studying.

He walks into his bedroom, passing his bed, one end of which is raised up on concrete blocks. It's better for his back, he says, which still bothers him years after the accident. You get used to living with the pain, he says. One photograph on the wall shows him on graduation day, wearing a suit and tie, standing next to Julia in a dress. He says, "This, well, Julia Andrea with boots, makeup, let's say, I don't know, it was because we had graduated recently, I don't know, they wanted to take a picture. I don't know, but to go around like that was too much. She didn't like it."

Always playing at something, rejecting the more refined, Julia found it difficult to accept the complexities of life. A day at the beach, a moment of spontaneous dance in the library, this is how Luciano remembers Julia. She was delighted when Luciano gave her a bouquet of violets, and it meant more to her, he says, than a car or a house. She once promised him that when she established her medical practice, she would never charge her patients. It wouldn't be just, she said. Luciano doesn't know what would have happened if Julia had been given the chance to test her ideals against the realities of life, if the military had given her the opportunity to live.

These are snapshots of a smiling Julia, always happy on the walls of Luciano's kitchen. There were times, Luciano recalls, when Julia was depressed, when she doubted herself. Sometimes, on final exam days, he asked her, "Are you ready?" and she said, "No, I don't think so." She was nervous and drank half a glass of wine to calm herself. Then Luciano said, "Come on," and they got on his motor scooter and went to the university, both of them invariably passing the exam at the top of the class.

Luciano has hung his scooter helmet on the wall next to the refrigerator, atop an old steering wheel, for some reason that only he understands. The helmet is stuffed with yellowed newspaper clippings reporting one of the many pardons that President Raúl Alfonsín and then President Carlos Menem issued, freeing all military officers accused of human rights violations during the Dirty War.

Luciano shows photographs of Julia at the zoo, trying to stick her hands through the bars to touch the animals. He remembers that the giraffe and Julia didn't both fit in the lens of their tiny camera, so Julia lured the giraffe with a branch to make it lower its head to her, and Luciano took the photograph. He says, "We'd go to the zoo, but it made us sad for all the prisoners there. The pumas . . . they weren't free." Luciano laughs for a moment and says again, "The animals were prisoners." He pauses, then goes on to some other subject.

Perhaps Luciano doesn't like the zoo because it reminds him of his brother, Andrés, who was a political prisoner for eight years. Andrés had been a Montonero, a member of an illegal Marxist organization during the 1970s. The Montoneros, embracing the broad spectrum of opponents to the military state, ranged from Marxist intellectuals to armed combatants, fellow travelers, and terrorists. The military was intent on exterminating all traces of the Montoneros because, for them, there was little difference between the bomb-throwing assassin and the armchair sympathizer. A Montonero was an enemy of the state. Therefore, for their work in Villa María in petitioning for improved medical conditions for the poor and more access to higher education, Andrés and a group of about a dozen other adolescents were arrested.

In some respects, Andrés and his companions can be considered the more fortunate political prisoners because they had been arrested during the brief period of democracy following Perón's return. This meant that even after the military took over in the 1976 coup, official prisoners could not be made to disappear from the register without forcing the Junta to admit there was in place a clandestine system, parallel to the official courts, that dealt with political opponents. Therefore, for eight years, while the repression targeted all types of Argentines—terrorists, priests, children, and revolutionaries—Andrés and the other Montoneros in his group were held in safety by their sworn enemy, the State.

That is not to say that Andrés's stay in prison was an altogether pleasant one. He spent part of his sentence in La Cuarenta, close to his family's house in Villa María, a prison once rated as having the lowest living conditions in Argentina and quite possibly the worst official prison in all of Latin America. Designed for a maximum capacity of seven hundred, it held, at its most crowded level, over two thousand. Moreover, the state security apparatus, in an attempt to break contact between prisoners and their family members, was constantly transferring prisoners to different installations all across Argentina.

It was a time when many families of political prisoners gave up, ceding victory to the military. They were unable to bear up under the emotional strain of traveling the width and breadth of Argentina on the hint of news of a new prison transfer. This was not, however, the case with Luciano, who took a decisive role.

Luciano was a young neurosurgeon, still in medical school, and at the top of his class. He had received the highest grades on the entrance exam at the best hospital in Córdoba, and in his daily conversations with his instructors, he was addressed as *vos*, the informal Argentine "you," instead of the formal *usted*. Luciano seemed destined to enter and rise rapidly through the ranks of the hospital.

Luciano, however, risked his career and his life to participate in the political prisoner assistance group. In this loosely formed Peronist organization, Luciano volunteered to smuggle the political news to his brother's group in jail. Each week, Luciano summed up the national and international news on a thin sheet of paper and smuggled it in a cigarette package past the guards. Soon afterwards, Luciano decided that it was too dangerous to use the cigarette method, and he pulled out one of his teeth. He explains casually, "It had always been loose." He rolled the note into a wad and inserted it into the space left in his gum, this way bringing news to his brother.

But these are memories of the person Luciano used to be, the clear thinker, the decisive risk-taker. As his mother often remarks, it is one of the family's greater ironies that Luciano, once so capable and willing to help other people, should now be hardly able to help himself, lost in the smoke and vapor of his thoughts.

As far as Luciano can remember, Julia never participated in any of his political activities. She knew what was going on, of course, but she was an observer of events, not an active participant. This was not the case with Luciano's ex-wife, from whom he used to hide even the fact that he was writing to his brother. She was of a different "political persuasion" he says, and she wouldn't have understood.

Luciano doesn't know how it came about that he and Julia broke up. One day, he just came to the conclusion that their relationship had been running on inertia instead of real feeling for too long, and, after more than eight years of going out with Julia, he decided that they shouldn't see each other anymore. Julia was crushed by his rejection; she hadn't felt that things had been going so badly and she was still very much in love. Luciano, however, began dating another woman doctor at the hospital, and, a short time afterwards, they married and had two children. It was not a happy marriage, and he soon divorced.

But if one were to look at all of the mementos and photographs spread throughout his house, one would never know that almost twenty years had passed since the day Luciano broke up with Julia. There are no pictures of his ex-wife, his children, or his family, nothing to show that he had had a life after Julia. There are only pictures of Luciano and Julia, lining room after room in his cavernous house. He tells stories only of Julia. In showing a stack of photos from the old days, Luciano accidentally comes across scenes from his wedding party, which he quickly flips through, looking for pictures of Julia. "Not a day goes by," he says, "when I don't think of her," and he seems to think of nothing else.

The last artifact that Luciano attempts to explain is a surrealistic painting nailed to the wall of his bedroom. It was a present from Julia, a poster advertising the 1967 modern art exhibition in Córdoba. He admits that for months he couldn't make any sense of it, its wavy black lines and orange blotches a complete chaos to him. But he kept the picture because it came from her. As the days passed, he realized that if he backed up, almost going through the doorway of the adjoining room, he could begin to see an order to the picture. The random lines formed a mustache, eyebrows, a jagged cheek—the face of a man begins to emerge, painted from the perspective of a room away.

At first, there seems to be little substance in Luciano's random monologue. He is incomprehensible in his ramblings, and one can never be sure of what it was he said, or what it was he meant to say. But all that he does say, jumbled and confused, all the things he's kept, the photographs and yellowed newspaper clippings that fill his house, are all a part of Julia, the way in which he understands her. She might have been kidnapped. She might have been tortured and killed, but for Luciano she never really disappeared.

As he lies down on his bed, adjusting the pillows around him, his back throbbing in pain, he turns to the picture of Julia on his bed stand—carefully positioned so he can see her face—smiles, and turns off the light.

María Isabel Chorobik de Mariani

Founder of Abuelas de la Plaza de Mayo (Grandmothers of the Plaza de Mayo), human rights organization dedicated to the search of the children of the disappeared.

Abuelas started with me in 1976, when a group of mothers came about, demanding the return of their children in the Plaza de Mayo. I didn't know about the existence of this group, as much as I didn't know anything about the reality of what was really happening in the country. Everything was controlled by the military government. I didn't have an idea that children, grandchildren, that people were disappearing. I was a professor at this time, and I knew that they were killing many people, students of mine. I knew what was happening in the newspapers, the horrors, but I didn't realize that people were disappearing. I didn't know. That news didn't come out. I believed that they were killing people, and that was the drama and the horror that I was living, that was what was happening. But nothing more.

In my case, they murdered my daughter-in-law in her house and took away my granddaughter. They didn't take away my son because he had just left the house. They killed him nine months afterward. All of this happened in the house of my daughter-in-law and my son on November 24, 1976. First I thought that the child was dead. Yes, I knew that Diana, my daughter-in-law, was dead. So I knew that I didn't have to look for Diana, although they wouldn't return her body. I thought that the child was dead. Yes, I gave the child up as dead and cried desperately. I went insane, but, more or less a month afterwards, I had the total assurance that the child was alive, that she had been taken alive.

I began to look for her, but without knowing where or how. I was in a different world which we were all in. Who could know how to proceed in a case like this? No one. So I was going around, I went looking in the neighborhood. No one wanted to say anything. Moreover, it was something important. The Armed Forces mounted a really big attack on the house, in such a way that they removed all of the people. And no one saw anything? And the rumors were those that the very policemen and soldiers who took them had spread. Someone asked me, "Why don't you go to the juvenile court?" It hadn't occurred to me to go to the juvenile court. I went there, and I began with the police, of course. I stuck myself in the middle of it, without knowing that there were concentration camps in certain police stations. I went. I stuck myself in there, alone. They let me go in. I think that I was saved by pure miracle.

I would have disappeared. One day I even went to the Comisaría Quinta in La Plata. They asked me, "What do you want?" I had brought a letter along with me in case the police didn't receive me. And they brought me to the police commissioner, because a person who knew the commissioner had given me information. So I went there. There were a lot of people there; I didn't know why they were crying. Couples. There were women who were crying continuously. They made all of them leave at the point of a gun, and because I had brought the letter, they let me, alone, stay. And they made me go through where, I found out later, the cells were. I spoke with the commissioner, and of course he told me that the child was still alive, but if I said so he would deny it for the rest of his life. He told me all this because of the friend who had sent me with the letter. He told me, "Go, look in such and such a place." I didn't know whom to talk with. I didn't know any policemen. He told me to go to the Regional, and I didn't even know where it was.

And I was where the disappeared were, in the cells, without knowing it. They ordered me about, they made me go, took me out, took me over there, directing me with their bayonet. And, well, I left and tried to find out where this place was, but it was impossible. They denied me everything, everything. But I want to say that I put myself in the mouth of the wolf. I was completely ignorant. They could have locked me up, they could have killed me, anything, there. I hadn't told anyone at home that I was going there.

Well, one day I was on one of my trips to the lawyer's office for minors, and an assistant was attending me, a woman who I always say was the real founder of Abuelas, Dr. Pegenaute. She told me, "Señora, you're not the only one who's looking. There are two other women who are also looking for little children."

"What?" I said. "Two more women?" I thought I was alone. I asked her if I could have the address of one of these grandmothers who she said is looking for her grandchild. She gave me the address immediately, and there Abuelas was born. I went to the house of Alicia de la Cuadra. I rang the doorbell at eleven o'clock in the morning, and I left there at five o'clock in the afternoon.

She told me what was really going on, what I had been ignorant of. She said that she knew that her pregnant daughter was in the Quinta. She knew that her daughter was a prisoner in the Comisaría Quinta! She was looking for her granddaughter because she had received a message that a baby girl had been born. She was called Elena. It was one of the very few cases in which a message arrived.

A few days later, Alicia told me that all of the mothers were going to turn in a document concerning their case, and that if I wanted to prepare my case, and if I wanted to go with her, I could turn in my document. That is to say, with tremendous fear and anxiety of not knowing how to do these things, I wrote up the history of my case, and I brought that little paper.

I don't know how we found the strength. I had an old typewriter that I think Christopher Columbus brought with him when he arrived. Extremely old. On this machine, I wrote my document, including the documents for the child, the parents, all that had happened. I took the paper with me. We went with Alicia, and there I met a group of mothers who had disappeared children, and some of these mothers—ten of them—had pregnant daughters, and they were looking for their daughters. At this moment, they were looking for their children. There wasn't a group to look for children. There, I was lucky enough to meet the founder of the Mothers, Azucena Villaflor, who later disappeared.

She was there. It was the first time that I met her. And, well, afterwards I met other mothers, grandmothers, all with their papers. And one thing surprised me: the serenity that they displayed. They've always had this serenity, even up to today. Even up to today it still seems a marvel, the serenity that the majority of the women have—I would say ninety-nine percent of them. I remember one of the grandmothers, Neuhaus, with a great big beautiful smile, didn't say anything to me, but welcomed me with a smile. I was accustomed in those days that everyone would cross the sidewalk in front of me in order not to see me because I was contagious. And I was surprised by the sensation of peace that they all had, considering their pain and desperation. They were calm.

And, well, we got together under a tree in La Plaza San Martín in Buenos Aires. It was filled with soldiers, with policemen, dogs, weapons everywhere—for me, it was quite new. I had never seen this. It was such a novelty that I didn't know what to do. The women shouted, asked for the return of their children, and I, I was silent, and I remained with the paper in my hand. And then, this government representative arrived, and they all went with their papers. Then a short, chubby little woman came to me and she said, "Did you give your paper?" "No, I have it here." And she took it out of my hand and, running among the dogs and the weapons and the soldiers, she reached this man and gave him my paper. I'm never going to forget her. I only saw her one more time. She disappeared almost right away. They took her away.

Before we left, each one going to her place, I told them my story. Each one knew the story of the other. Then I told them that I thought the children should be looked for in a certain way, in other places. And I asked them what they thought if we wrote a letter to the Pope. It occurred to me to write to the Pope. (He was from Krakow, like my parents.) Of course, the Pope didn't care, and, well, we decided to meet the next week with many precautions, in the house of one of us.

I used to ride in the car with my husband. I didn't even know how to take a bus. I didn't know the area. It was only a short period of time since I had moved to this house because the military destroyed mine the night they took my son. And there was a very active little woman who said, "Are you going to the meeting in La Plata?" "Yes." "Let's go together. And where do you live?" "I live on Lacroze Street." "Well, I live a block from you." It was Hebe Bonafini, later president of the Madres. We met with the grandmothers and we decided to write letters to certain people. I tell you that I have a folder filled with I don't know how many letters. I wrote the letters on this old machine of mine. And we all signed, each one of us. I used to bring them, hidden, and we would meet in a café or in the house of one of them, like we were celebrating a birthday in the cafés, and there we signed the papers that we sent, to politicians, abroad, all around the world. And we went to all the courts in the province and outside of Buenos Aires.

I can't explain to myself how we found the strength. Sometimes we left here at seven o'clock in the morning, in wintertime, or on a terrible night, raining. We didn't realize that we were hungry, or that we were cold, or that it rained, nothing, until we had a hole in a shoe and we had to buy a new one, when we realized that it was leaking. It was like that.

I was with Abuelas until 1989, and we had received five thousand bits of information. It hurts you a lot that people don't understand the problem of the disappeared children, but, nevertheless, there are thousands of people who have helped us by passing on information. That is to say, you have to make a balance. You want so badly to have the grandchildren that you get angry when the people don't help.

There are about two hundred and fifty documented cases, but nothing's known about the children about whom a complaint was never made. That is to say, how many mothers, how many young wives, went to prison pregnant, and their mothers never knew? Many of the mothers and grandmothers who are in Abuelas didn't know that their daughters were pregnant. I believe that the figure is probably double. My calculation is that there are probably some four hundred children, among those, the documented ones. Up until I retired from Abuelas, there were some forty-nine children, but there are still a lot missing.

From the information that someone brings you, they tell you in this house, this place, there is a little child, a little girl that can be a *desaparecida*. Then you have to investigate, you have to find out if this first part is true. Afterward, what characteristics does this child have? Since what year has she been in this house? Anything that can demonstrate a matter of genetics, hobbies, tastes, height, build—such as photographs. Sometimes I've taken photographs, getting myself invited to a birthday party where this little girl is invited as well, one of the girls whom I was following. And take pictures there. One time I cut a little lock of hair because I thought that with the hair of this child—I had a lock of hair from my granddaughter—I could find out if it was her. Well, once we get this all put together, information about the false parents, the child, the birth, the school, the characteristics, once this is all ready, we go to the courts.

When we realized that we had to prove something almost unprovable, that's when I read in the newspaper *Día*, in La Plata, that there was a blood analysis by which it was possible to know to which family this child belonged, without the parents. So, each time we went to Europe, to the United Nations, wherever, we went to hospitals, blood banks, to see if someone could tell us what this analysis was all about. We got access to a doctor from the New York blood bank, a super-famous doctor who discovered how to prevent people from dying from R-negative. When we told him what we're looking for, he started making some calculations and said that it was possible.

A year or so later, I don't remember when, we were in New York again and they told us about the Society for the Advancement of Science that had answers, that it can be done, and that there was going to be a symposium in a few days to talk about this. The National Bank of Genetic Data is established in the Durán hospital, where our idea was for us to give blood samples there because we were conscious of the fact that we weren't going to find all of the children, but that one day these children could find their families.

Where was Julia's child taken? Into this sinister darkness where they threw the child, no? Because sometimes they gave them away upon being born, sometimes they left them two or three days. And I fear that more than once they killed them. The baby girls often went to policemen. The machismo of the military made them always look more for little boys. This is perhaps the reason why we have found more girls than boys. We have more access to the police because they live in the regular neighborhoods. They're more among the people. But the military have their own neighborhoods. When we've followed the trail of a child, almost always a little boy, the investigation dies in the neighborhood because we can't get in there.

Where could Julia's child be? It occurred to me that she was in the place where she was born or given or sold to the police. Generally the godfather of this child that we are looking for is a policeman, and generally this policeman was the one that gave or sold the child to these people. When they bring us information about a child being born on such and such a date, we take into account a range of three months before and three months after the date of birth, thinking that it could have been a premature birth or it could have been late, or that they wrote the date later on. Many times the name Montesini has come up, but nothing has ever come of it.

With the warped mentality of the kidnappers, you can never put yourself in their place. You can't think like them. But it has to do with why they raised them. It wasn't out of affection. Is it in order to make the child of a political activist into a soldier, in order to make him a torturing policeman? I have asked myself this so many nights that I haven't been able to sleep, wondering why. I haven't reached a conclusion, because we can't think like them. But without a doubt, it wasn't out of solidarity or generosity. This damned person General Camps is my number one enemy because he's the one that took away my granddaughter. He knows where she is. I have the name of the person who took the child out of her mother's arms. This dreadful person takes children away from their parents and gives them to families who could "raise them well." It could be messianism. It could be messianism. But affection for the children? It's something dirty, very morbid.

One time, some grandparents who live outside of Buenos Aires came. 1986, I think it must have been. And they brought me a letter that their daughter had sent them from a concentration camp in which she told them of a baby girl she had had and that she was called such and such. And I said, with this in hand, now, you give it to us after six years, seven years? And the father looked at me with eyes filled with tears, and he said, "We were afraid." And this was the first time that I had a notion of what this fear meant to the people. I believe that I changed my critical spirit, because I used to be very critical of the people who didn't have the courage to do things. I changed because I understood. The terror did this. It could be the fear that the people had that silenced them. But there are also many fascists here. I prefer to think that it's fear.

V I I I

Victoria

Years of smoking and speaking her mind give Victoria a hoarse cough as she talks. She remembers meeting Julia the day they applied, for residency together at the Children's Hospital of Córdoba in 1973. They were among the two hundred medical students who waited in the hallway, with fear and trembling, on the benches outside the examining room. After what had seemed like endless years of medical school, they finally had a chance to practice their profession, and it all depended on that one, terrible, personal interview. Of two hundred applicants, twenty entered the hospital that day, including Victoria and Julia, and a friendship formed between the two aspiring doctors that would last until Julia's disappearance, and even beyond. Victoria recalls:

> When we entered residency, we were chosen for the night shift. We were together in the room when we were chosen for the shift.

We had a shift every forty-eight hours, and I had guard duty with Julia. And Julia was very gentle. She was very fair-skinned, had very clear eyes, a voice that had nothing to do with my tone of voice; rather, it was a very gentle voice, melodious. I'm a Scorpio, and she's a Scorpio as well.

That is to say, we were both born in November. . . . We had many characteristics in common. What happened is that I'm more of an extrovert, you see.

If they were born under the same stars, Victoria's was the rising and Julia's the descending. Victoria was the talker. She would enter a room full of people and immediately strike up a conversation, telling them what she wanted to say, and if they didn't like it, well, that was their problem. But Julia, she recalls, was much different. At first, she didn't seem to relate well to people. She was distant, and it was harder for her to find a way to interact. Victoria lived for the smell of battle. Julia practiced the art of compromise. Where Victoria pushed ahead, Julia waited, thinking, debating how she should proceed. In a way, Victoria explains, "she was a person whom you would call an introvert, a person whose life passed disappearing among the group."

But Julia had her own way of handling a situation, of interacting with people, not as spontaneously as Victoria, but she had a way about her that won people over and instilled confidence. As Victoria says:

It's tremendously difficult to define Julia because, first of all, I don't want to make poetry out of her. She was a direct person, for example; that is to say, if she had to tell you something, she was going to tell you. She wasn't going to turn around, nor was she the kind of person who would talk behind people's backs. And she was a person who found it difficult to connect herself with someone. But when she connected, she gave a lot. She was the kind of person who would give more than receive. She was always there when you needed her.

All in all, Victoria describes her residency at the hospital as "a beautiful time." Everything was new and exciting. They were doctors at last, or at least doctors in residency. Theirs was a difficult job, with long hours and often little consideration from the permanent staff, but they were finally completing their dreams, and they were doing it together. Victoria remembers how, when they got off from their shift on Sunday mornings, not having slept for two days, she and Julia went straight to the beach close by the hospital. And all their friends who were off at the same time came with them. They had barbecues on the beach, played soccer, sang songs. "It was a group that wasn't just work," Victoria recalls. "We did absolutely everything together."

They had their careers, and more—there was a feeling of solidarity, a feeling of belonging at the hospital that seemed to flow through their group. They had chosen medicine because it fascinated them. They had chosen to work in the state hospital because they wanted to help the children from the poor barrios, the underprivileged, not just to talk social justice but to practice it. There were, however, drawbacks to working at the hospital in Córdoba and dangers in being a doctor in residency. As Victoria explains, it was not just one big party at the beach:

> Children's doctors were characterized as being Trotskyist doctors. This was not the case. We were persecuted. To be a doctor in residency at that time was to put a sign on yourself that said "militant." Because you were a person who thought, someone who worked for the community. If we could go to work in the marginalized slums, in *la villa*, if we could run literacy programs for the people, then we ran literacy programs. A "doctor in residency" was another name for someone who thought, and someone who thought wasn't worth anything.

As profound changes began to take place in Peronist splinter organizations, leftist terrorism started on one side and right-wing death squads were forming on the other, and the type of persecution the doctors in residence faced was becoming frighteningly clear. In 1975, a group of armed unionists took control of the children's hospital, instilling terror as they searched through the rooms, throwing out doctors and patients alike. They had come looking for certain Peronist doctors whom they said were subversive. Victoria remembers standing outside the hospital after having been forced out, watching sadly as armed hooligans rummaged through the hospital unchecked by local police. The next day, a daily newspaper in Córdoba described the incident as a group of Trotskyist doctors having taken the hospital by storm. The campaign of misinformation and violence directed against the young doctors had begun.

That year, two doctors from the hospital were murdered, one literally cut in half by machine gun fire in the doorway of his house as his wife and young child looked on. Officially, these were considered as isolated incidents, and there was no talk of government involvement. However, it was understood that it was the military, now almost visibly propping up the civilian government, using groups such as these unionists to rid themselves unofficially of "enemies of the state," the list of which soon included anyone working in the decidedly "subversive" fields of anthropology, sociology, and popular medicine.

Still, among the bloodshed and the terror, the doctors at the children's hospital continued to struggle for their vision of a more just society. Victoria describes herself and Julia as part of "a group, a generation that began to realize the rights that it had, not the right to be rich but rather the right to exist, the right to raise a family, the right to education for your children." The doctors sometimes worked ninety-six hour weeks, pulling overtime, submerging themselves in medicine. For them, the hospital wasn't just a place to where the sick could come. It was also the place to form assemblies and to debate the state of the health care system. They demanded wage increases from the government, improved work conditions. The doctors were militants in this sense, Victoria admits, but they

> weren't bomb throwers. They were militants like if you join a party and form part of a committee and, well, take to the streets, carrying the party's flag. It didn't matter if you were a Peronist and another doctor was a Radical and another a Conservative— all were united in the struggle so that a doctor in the hospital could maintain a family.

In the middle of her residency, a physical change began to take place in Julia. She tired easily, became fatigued. Her workload was difficult, but it had always been that way; she didn't see why it would be too much for her now. She didn't know what was happening, and she was worried. Soon she couldn't walk ten meters without having trouble breathing. She described her condition to Victoria, and together they went to a specialist. At first, the doctors thought Julia might have tuberculosis, but this was soon dismissed. As Julia's condition worsened, Victoria and another companion took Julia for a second opinion. They found that Julia had a serious problem with one of her heart valves. She was receiving a dangerously low level of oxygen, and the valve needed to be replaced.

The Montesini family didn't have the money for such an expensive operation, and Victoria went about the hospital collecting money, asking colleagues, friends, to contribute something, anything, to save Julia's life. Victoria even went so far as to take out credits from lending institutions to finance the operation.

In November 1975, the operation was performed successfully. Julia's health began to improve markedly in the following year, and she continued having regular checkups at the nearby cardiac unit to control her condition. It was at this hospital that she met her future husband, Alberto Espinoza, one of the young resident doctors specializing in cardiology.

(One of the many ironies of the situation is that after Julia had been taken away and was languishing in a secret detention center, the bills for her heart operation still had to be paid and the loans paid back. Victoria, therefore, took it upon herself to pay the remaining bills, to clear up Julia's debts. It was the one last act of love for a friend whom she would never see again.)

Victoria recalls vividly the day they took Julia. She was on guard duty in Adrogué, a city close to where Julia was working, when she received a phone call from a friend of hers called Ester. "She called me, telling me, 'Look, they took Julia and Alberto. Don't go home. . . . Go somewhere else.' Really, it was like that. We didn't know where she was, who was going to be next."

Victoria didn't know what to do. She was shocked, but she knew enough not to go home, fearing that if Julia could be made to disappear, so could she. With good reason she was afraid. Later she learned that when Alberto had been taken, various articles from the house had been taken also, including photographs of Julia's wedding in which Victoria appeared prominently. To be seen in a photograph with a disappeared person was proof of fraternizing with a "subversive" and a telling sign that she was most probably a terrorist as well.

After the initial shock, it was the randomness of the kidnappings that troubled Victoria. Yes, the kidnappings of Alberto and Julia were well coordinated. One hour apart, they had obviously been planned with precision. But it could just as easily have been Julia to receive the phone call, telling her that Victoria had been taken. That was what disturbed her most. They were all part of the same group. One didn't seem more militant than the other. Because of their health campaigns in the poor neighborhoods, because of their asking for wage increases, literacy programs, they had imagined that some retaliation by the government was possible. Now, it had finally happened, and they were all in danger. Who would be next?

Victoria spent several days in houses of friends, afraid to go back home, even to collect her clothes. One day Victoria decided to go back, hoping to snatch a few of her belongings and hurry back to the safe house. She was with her family that day and had been playing with her three-year-old nephew. As she went out the door, he began to cry because she wouldn't let him come along. In order to comfort her nephew, Victoria took him with her, an act she later regretted.

Victoria was upstairs, cramming some things into a bag when she heard the police sirens. She stopped, listening, silent, as the sirens came closer. Fearing that they had come to take her just as they had taken Julia, fearing that her nephew would be taken as well, she took her nephew onto the balcony and, reaching out, placed him on the roof of a nearby neighbor's house. Telling the little boy to keep quiet and wait for her, Victoria ran out of the house, hoping that if they kidnapped her she would be far enough away so that he wouldn't be found.

As Victoria ran, crisscrossing the streets, she soon realized that the police sirens had not been indicating her capture. They passed by her house without stopping, off to pursue some other target. Victoria paused to breathe deeply. She knew that she was safe. But then she remembered the little boy stranded on the rooftop. Her heart pounding, frantic, she returned to the house to find her nephew crying, but safe, where she had left him. She grabbed the child and her belongings and rushed out of the house. Victoria now says she is thankful that memory is such a strange device, selective and inexact, because her nephew, now grown up, has no recollection of those few terrifying minutes when his aunt left him on the rooftop alone.

After the fear for her own safety had subsided and she believed that she could resume her life again, Victoria returned to the hospital. There, among her colleagues, she began to find the courage to write to the medical union and to the medical school, protesting the disappearance of Julia and Alberto. She asked any of Julia's friends if they knew a policeman, a soldier, or a Church official to find out what had happened; tried to make contacts; tried to find out what branch of the military had taken the Montesinis; tried to find out where they were being held.

There was never any official response; no one admitted to knowing who had taken Julia. Just as Julia's mother, Catalina, had often been told, they said it was most probably a terrorist act by the left wing or, if the government had taken them, then they must have been taken for a reason. What was her name again? Victoria should call back later.

Several years passed, and Victoria still didn't know what had happened to Julia. The worst of the repression had died down, people weren't being taken in such large numbers anymore, and some prisoners were beginning to be released. The rebellion in the north had effectively ceased to exist. Fragmented rumors arose of concentration camps and torture, but nothing more than rumors, and nothing was ever said publicly. The military government exercised complete control and still maintained that there were no political prisoners in Argentina.

Victoria clung to the hope that Julia had somehow escaped or had been released, that she was living in exile somewhere, unable, or too afraid, to write. It was this hope that kept Victoria and many other friends of Julia from recognizing the truth of what was going on around them, of even contemplating it. A state-led machine of mass brutality and assassination was the unthinkable thought, too terrible to be believed.

In 1980 Victoria went to Europe. It was there that she found friends who had escaped from Argentina by boat to nearby Uruguay, or who had smuggled themselves into Brazil, before leaving for Europe. It was a wonderful experience, she says, to see so many people still alive whom she thought had been killed.

But what about Julia? Was she there? Was Alberto? Wherever she found groups of expatriate Argentines, in Spain, Italy, France, Germany, or Switzerland, she asked about Julia. Had anyone seen her? Was she close by? They had to tell her. She had to know. She couldn't stop until she found something, some bit of information. But no one had the answers to Victoria's questions, and, as time passed, she stopped asking them. As Victoria admits:

> Although it might appear to be a lie to you, there comes a moment when you lower your arms, when you don't struggle anymore, when you don't believe, when you don't believe in hope, so that it doesn't hurt you as much after you realize the truth. Well, it was like that. It was like that, I don't know, a necessity to conform.

Victoria didn't go to Julia's funeral. She says that she had a lot of work to do at the hospital, that she couldn't leave her patients behind. She still works hard to make a decent living, very hard, she explains. After over twenty years of experience as a full-time pediatrician, she makes about $6,000 a year. Sometimes, to earn a bit of extra money, she even lends a hand at her mother's clothing boutique. Working at the state hospital still doesn't pay well, but she continues to put in the long hours, dedicating herself to medicine, to the children. The Dirty

War couldn't take away her passion for life, nor could it take away her memories. She still remembers Julia, and she still guards within her a large reservoir of anger for those who murdered her. But as for hope, after all these years, there isn't any left.

VOICE 8

Dr. Jorge Reinaldo Vanossi

*Representative in the Argentine Chamber of Deputies, the
Union Civica Radical (Radical Civic Union); author and
lecturer on the role of democracy in Latin American
society and the Argentine constitution.*

It wasn't as if there were the presence of occupying countries, such as
the four triumphal powers that created a trial in Germany after the
World War. Here was no type of occupying power, no pressure. The
trials of the Junta were simply the spontaneous decision of the Argentine Congress and President Alfonsín.

Today, the pardon that President Menem issued has created disorder because it gives the impression that everything has been forgotten
and everything has been forgiven. In other words, it's as if it's all
worth the same: obey the law or not obey the law. There is no refer-

ence point, that which sociologists call "a state of anonymity," where there are no parameters. There is no normative point that permits one to distinguish legality from illegality. This is a bad example for the coming generations, and, in some way, it is a stimulus so that if the conditions repeat themselves, what happened will be repeated as well.

We always said that the fundamental accusation against the Junta was the repressive methodology, the repressive procedure, the completely violent way in which the law was tossed aside, without judges. There were simply de facto executions or disappearances. If there had been at least a law tribunal that, with its signature, assumed the responsibilities, it would have been a different thing altogether.

The members of the Junta are characters from the past who have been judged by public opinion, but, sadly, they act with this boldness, this pride, because it's shown that there has been no type of repentance, no type of recognition of their mistakes. We, paraphrasing a sentence of a famous Argentine writer, said that the fight against cannibals can permit many things except eating the cannibals. Because if, in the fight against the cannibals, we eat the cannibals, we transform ourselves into maneaters, and we lose any type of moral justification. That is to say, if there existed this guerrilla phenomenon in the country, terrorists, subversives, the state should have suffocated it by legal means, through constitutional means, not by divorcing itself from the law. That is to say that this so-called state terrorism signified in some way applying the Machiavellian criteria with which the end justifies the means. Therefore, all of the means were made ready to achieve this end. And this is really what deserves reproach and was the object of . . . the criminal prosecution of the *comandantes*.

It's all documented in the book *Nunca Más* that the National Commission on the Disappearance of People published, in which hundreds of witnesses testified, in which there is an infinite quantity of documentary, testimonial proof of all sorts.

If the political parties become discredited, if there's a large loss in the trust of the political class, then this free, light, happy, oblivion can create the rebirth of the military myth, of the myth that portrays the military as saviors of the fatherland and as architects of order, which is fundamentally the image that they cultivated for quite a long time. It's dangerous because it might be the seed that can grow into the new plant of militarism in Argentina. The tree of militarism can grow up again. At this moment, the conditions aren't right because, obviously, the constitutional system and open elections provide a channel for the dissatisfaction and hopes and anxieties through a political party.

I believe that the present government doesn't have a plan to write a lucid history of the Dirty War, moreover, this pardon has produced a sensation of "Well, let's not talk about this subject any more." It has already produced an effect on public opinion because polls by Gallup and other agencies indicate that, among the important issues that preoccupy Argentine opinion, the subject of human rights is really, really low. It holds a minimum percentage.

President Menem doesn't talk about the subject. There is a cloak of silence, a kind of silence of an accomplice. He doesn't apologize for the repression. He was also held prisoner, so he can't apologize for the repression. He simply doesn't talk about it. If you see the analyses newspapers have made concerning what subjects the president talks about, the subject most talked about is presidential election, the subject that concerns him most personally.

The dictatorship was connected with other dictatorships, including supposedly constitutional governments, but really authoritarian, such as Stroessner in Paraguay. It also had contact with the military dictatorship in Uruguay, and it is supposed that many disappearances of people were done with some type of complicity or cover-up by the military authorities in other countries: Brazil, Uruguay, Paraguay, Chile, especially the bordering countries. For example, proof is going to come out now, when the files of the Stroessner government are opened up in Paraguay. Proof that the secret police of Stroessner collaborated in an exchange of prisoners with the Argentine police is already emerging. But who knows how many years it's going to take before it's cleared up?

I believe that the title of the book, *Nunca Más* [*Never Again*], indicates what the desire and the aspiration of the Argentine people are.

That is to say, we don't want situations such as these ever to be repeated. This is a long history of violence gradually becoming so powerful all over the country, and the military coups d'état, as the name indicates, militarized the state, made it a state composed of force, and the phenomenon of the guerrilla, the phenomenon of subversive militarization, lent the society its martial tone. That is to say, there was a hardening of both poles in the society and in the state.

And this brought about the climax of tension that led to the collective massacre because, obviously, there were excesses on one side and excesses on the other. And each one justified the other. In the end, it gave the impression that they fed each other reciprocally, because the guerrillas justified themselves by the actions of the army, and the army justified themselves by the actions of the guerrillas. It was a type of reciprocal justification. This brought about a level of moral insanity in the Republic, which little by little the society is now trying to overcome. I think that there's a different type of social valuation. In their time, the coups d'état were approved of. Today, if someone speaks about a coup, this is anathema, it is punishable. The de facto governments that commanded by decree, that dissolved parties, intervened in the judicial system, were tolerated. Today, no one would attempt to justify a heresy such as this.

The people don't talk about this subject of the disappeared. Very few. They are the minority. Even the common people don't talk about this subject, which is quite significant. The people are pressured by immediate needs, the cost of living, unemployment, the problem with the public schools, the retirement system. These are the subjects, the issues, that concretely touch the people today. The people, in their mental space, in their mental system, dedicate most of their time to these problems.

I X

Francisco

Francisco was one of the senior doctors who interviewed Julia the day she applied for residency at the Children's Hospital of Córdoba. He is the director now and has been for many years. He apologizes for not having much time to talk about the past, but he has a hospital to run. He can spare an hour for a quick chat, however, and he calls his secretary to bring in coffee and croissants. He remembers that first interview clearly, he says, including the questions that he asked Julia:

> Well, we made the selection and chose who were going to enter. I don't remember how the dialogue went, but we asked, apart from pediatrics, what other type of interests you had, if you liked, I don't know, painting or music, literature. And she said, "I learned folk dances." And I asked her a question she didn't know how to answer. There's an Argentine folk dance called *la condición*

(it comes from the minuet). So I asked her the origin of the dance, and she didn't know.

Another examining doctor got angry because I was asking questions that didn't have anything to do with—well I don't know why he got angry. But this is one aspect of her personality, something that one doesn't usually show.

Apart from this one anecdote and one or two other brief recollections, Francisco says that he has a very unclear idea of who this young doctor named Julia was. He has a more generalized memory of the late seventies, of the conditions that affected the entire medical community at Córdoba, and of the politics of the hospital. After all, he says, "I had the same relationship with the rest of the doctors in residency" as with Julia. Doctors came. Doctors left. The residents formed part of the larger hospital, but they still remained separate from the administration.

A difference could be felt, Francisco explains, among the older and younger generations at the hospital. The administrators with their three-piece suits, tie pins, and formal grammar, were often scandalized by these youngish doctors in tennis shoes and blue jeans, bringing with them the radicalization of the seventies, social reform, and rock and roll. The doctors in residency spoke of politics, a new government, even the return of Perón. This last possibility was anathema to the older doctors, who still had fresh memories of *la Revolución Libertadora* in 1955 when Perón was overthrown, and the many years afterward when the official Peronist march couldn't be sung, the flag couldn't be waved, and Perón's name couldn't even be said in public. As Perón's return from exile became a distinct possibility, and the prohibited politics unearthed, it was the young doctors who were quick to take up his rhetoric of social justice and apply it to their studies of medicine.

The older doctors still warned that the business of the hospital was medicine, something that should not be confused with politics. Francisco says that the doctors in residency were always talking about some new movement, some social change:

They talked about politics, about anything. Medicine was politicized. The unionists were politicized, all of the student activity. The university was very, very politicized. And then the kids, that is to say the new residents, were very politicized; and in the assembly—they had a permanent assembly in order to discuss political topics. I attended very little. I never had any political militancy, and I didn't like the fact that it was politicized so much.

Francisco wasn't upset that the young doctors, including the soft-spoken Julia, participated in the assemblies. He imagines that it must have been an enriching experience for her and the other residents, a place where Peronists, Maoists, Radicals, pro-Soviets, and Conservatives could have a forum to discuss their differing points of view. What bothered him, however, was the way in which the doctors conducted themselves at the assembly, as well as what they demanded there. The point at which he could stand no more was when they asked for a pay raise for those working night shift, and some even proposed a strike:

And then this was, I believe, the first time that I intervened in the assembly, that I intervened amid the shouting. I had a lot of authority, because I was the instructor of the residents. If you take care of bicycles or cars, like a mechanic, you can have a strike or demand more money for fixing a car. But I believe that if you're a doctor, the same as if you're a priest, your first objective is—although what I'm telling you is mystical—to work for the rest. That is to say, I agree that all of us are employees or workers, and that we have to claim our rights, but in a way that the line isn't crossed after which the hospital is transformed into a battlefield.

Soon the hospital, as well as the rest of Córdoba, was transformed into a battlefield, although it wasn't because the doctors had demanded a pay raise. It was a combination of the myriad paramilitary groups cruising the streets and ransacking houses, snipers assassinating police officials, and the ever-present military, checking documents on the street corners and taking people away. No one was quite sure which group to blame for the increasing acts of violence, and, as Francisco recalls, the reaction to the violence from the people of Córdoba was extremely varied:

> There came a moment when there were so many bodies, for example, ten a day, fifteen a day, twenty a day. Every day the number was appearing in the newspapers because, moreover, the corpses weren't even identified. That is to say, you need to see the newspapers of the time. I remember that there were people who bet on how many would appear, the number of bodies, as if it were the lottery or bingo. One placed a bet of two and the other placed a bet of eighteen. And if you guessed right or if you came close, you won.

To people like Francisco, however, what was going on was no game. Perhaps it was because Francisco was Jewish and conscious of the persecution his people had faced during World World II that he recognized that the executions, the drive-by shootings, the sackings, didn't happen to "other people." He had no illusions that this terror had its boundaries. The next day he, or members of his family, might help to push the number up so that some lucky person might win the new lottery:

> We were afraid of going to sleep and not waking up. When I went to sleep in my house (I had two children, small ones) we turned up the radio or the television really loud so that you couldn't hear the machine guns, couldn't hear the bombs. I had put iron reinforcements on all the doors, both front and back. And I constantly used to walk around the house armed. When we used to see the sun, we felt freedom. Another day had passed that they hadn't killed us.

Francisco spent his nights in a vigil awash with fear, doubting that his family would live until dawn. For other fathers and mothers, the custom was to do the opposite, not to fear, not to pay attention to what was talked of in the newspapers, not to see what was going on in the streets. And when their neighbors were taken away, screaming in the night, that was the secret no one ever talked about. Many Argentines didn't want to see the disappeared as disappeared, but merely as detained, and when a person who had been disappeared was released, families of the "detained" hoped that the same would happen to their loved ones. They tried to convince themselves that nothing bad could ever happen to them, and they were encouraged in this delusion by the government officials, who, Francisco says, would say things like,

> "Calm down. At some time they're probably going to transport the prisoner to Mar de Plata, or to Campo de Mayo. Just relax, it's okay." Or, through the Church officials; high officials in the Church spoke with authorities in the army and afterward they told you, "Calm down."

The contradiction between the soothing words from the government and the stark sight of their children's empty beds at home brought a great deal of anguish to the families of the disappeared. It was an impossible dilemma. If they protested the disappearance, it could start a paper trail that would delay their son or daughter from being processed through the system, and it could quite possibly endanger their lives. On the other hand, if they decided to wait until their children were given back to them, without ever saying a word, they might be kept waiting forever. More than anything, Argentines wanted to believe that their sons and daughters were all right, that they would be coming home the next day or the day after. Because of this, they tried to keep the rising death toll on the periphery of their consciousness, tried not to think about how many had disappeared nor even imagine why so few ever seemed to come back. "Soon after," Francisco explains, "we didn't have a consciousness of the disappeared."

Oddly, it was in Europe and not in Argentina that Francisco became aware of the scope of the disappearances. In 1977, soon after Julia's disappearance, he traveled with his family to France, and he was immediately inundated with news from around the world, all of it relating to the Argentine disappeared. He remembers reading *Le Monde* and *Paris Match*, where there was talk of five thousand, eight thousand disappeared, figures Francisco had never seen before. Also, there were rumors of a list of disappeared people being compiled by the Vatican, which lent more credibility to the news. Argentine newspapers discussed the victims of terrorism and the young conscripts dying in the northern provinces at the hands of the godless revolutionaries, but military censorship made sure that there was no talk of the officially sanctioned murders, prison centers, and torture chambers run by the military.

In Paris, Francisco also began to understand the context of his own experience. He had made friends with an old man, also Jewish, who had escaped the Nazi death camps in World War II by living under an assumed name. Francisco remembers that as he began to tell the man of his experiences in Argentina, the man interrupted him:

> "Listen to me. When the sun comes up, don't you feel relief? Don't you feel how good it is to be alive?" And I said "Yes," because let's say that these things happened at night. It's typical of fascism (this occurred throughout the Second World War) and I remember when the sun comes up, I was relaxed, and he remembered exactly the same thing. And the sensation "I'm going to live one more day." It's not that now I'm saved. It's that I'm going to live one more day.

For Francisco, Naziism had been the archetype of persecution, not only for the Jews but also for all of humanity: it was the blueprint for terror. But as he continued talking to this old man, Francisco saw himself describing the same sensations, the same fears and anguish produced during the Holocaust, but it wasn't Europe in the 1930s and 1940s. It was Argentina, and it was now.

Because Francisco had become accustomed to the continual murders and kidnappings in Córdoba, their weight had been lost to him. Clusters of bodies on street corners had become part of his normal working day. Now, seated in a café in Paris, sipping coffee, quiet and relaxed, Francisco read the descriptions of violence with astonishment. He describes his experience in Córdoba as having been "put right in the middle of it. You were surrounded by trees, but you couldn't see the forest." But then he says:

It's not that I didn't know that there were disappeared, dead. Personally, they took my brother prisoner July 15, 1977, and on July 16, he hanged himself in the prison. It was the middle of *el Proceso*, surrounded by soldiers, in the prison where they had taken everyone prisoner. They came at night and took him away. They let his wife go free after he hanged himself in the prison. They came to find us. My brother hanged himself on July 16, at ten o'clock at night, and they came looking for me. I was in his house, sleeping, and in the morning police appeared all over the place with machine guns to tell me that my brother had committed suicide. I believe that he committed suicide; they made me identify the corpse. I know a lot about medicine, more than you might imagine. It was really credible that he had killed himself, because he didn't have one sign of violence, because he had the mark such as all hangings have, with a little bit of. . . .

Francisco cannot relate his story without stopping before the end. He starts with a smile, a clear, composed face, and he ends in tears. A few more words and the story is over, he can't go on. He thanks you for having listened, and then, with a firm handshake and a smile, he goes on about his work.

Francisco talks a lot about his own experiences, his doubts and his fears during the military government, and they are useful because they paint part of the background against which Julia's drama unfolds. But what is perhaps more important is what Francisco doesn't say. He doesn't talk much about Julia. He doesn't seem as if he's really able to talk about her because, as he insists, she is a blur, a dot among the graph of the incoming residents, one student among many. Through interviews with former colleagues and friends of Julia, however, it has been established that his portrayal of the past is not completely accurate.

What Francisco forgets to say or, rather, what he chooses not to remember is that he and Julia were close friends, that he was a friend of the Montesini family, that Julia knew his wife quite well, that Julia and Francisco used to go out together to eat, take walks after work. Francisco did not, as he insists, have the same relationship with Julia as with "the rest of the doctors in residency."

Many of Julia's friends interviewed for this investigation, those who went to great pains to reconstruct memories of her, deride Francisco for hiding his friendship. Up to a point, they can understand the defense and fear that he has built up after all these years, the realistic fear bred from a military that tortured and killed the person who stood up and said, "Yes, Julia was my friend." But the question they pose now is, "Why, after all these years, doesn't Francisco talk, why doesn't he at least try to reclaim a friendship that he abandoned in part out of fear and in part out of necessity?"

The answer is complex and can never be completely known, but a friend of Francisco has told me how desolated Francisco felt after the death of his brother. After being called down to identify his brother's corpse, after having to feel his throat to see if the rope marks had been caused by suicide or by foul play, Francisco said he wanted nothing more to do with the disappeared, that he didn't want to even think of them. If he was to forget the pain that his brother's death had caused him and his entire family, the anxiety and depression, then he had to forget Julia as well. Whatever Francisco's reasons, they are his alone.

Now, instead of guarding his house at night, Francisco guards his memory, keeping Julia under lock and key, pulling out only the few fragments of anecdotes that aren't too painful, that aren't too telling, of the friendship that once meant so much to him. When asked about Julia, he'll talk about a young girl, a doctor who once danced to folk music as a hobby. But nothing else. All the rest, his friendship, his late-night dinner conversations, lie hidden in the cupboard of memories. In this way, Francisco himself has disappeared, at least the Francisco who had once been Julia's friend, as have his hopes and her dreams, all of them swallowed up in the great denial.

VOICE 9

Luis Brandoni

*Popular actor in Argentine cinema and television; former
union representative; participant in Cultural Affairs in
the democratic government of Raúl Alfonsín (Asesor de
Cultura [ad honorem]).*

I became aware of the existence of the Alianza Anticomunista Argentina (Argentine Anti-Communist Alliance—AAA) by way of the newspapers. The AAA began to make their threats public. I was secretary
general of the Argentine Actors Association, the labor union that
brought together all of the actors in Argentina in such a way that we
realized what was going on.

The AAA was a paragovernmental/paramilitary organization, which
we all knew depended on the Minister of Social Welfare, José López
Rega, at this time a very influential man at the side of Perón who

carried out an important role. He came as Perón's secretary, as his minister as well. He was very reactionary, very crude. The night before Perón's return to the country, in the San Martín Municipal Theater, there was a group of municipal employees working there who belonged to López Rega's group, let's say the most reactionary part of Peronism, that was the seed of the AAA if it hadn't been formed yet.

I remember that many of my colleagues who were working in the San Martín on June 19 were told to be very careful on leaving the theater because they couldn't come back. What we knew was that the municipal workers were storing weapons in the San Martín theater. They were the weapons that on June 20 were brought to Ezeiza airport to repress the Peronists of the left, in the massacre at Ezeiza. I issued a formal complaint to the Ministry of the Interior that there were weapons in the theater.

The threats began as a message to society that there was going to be vigilante-style justice. The AAA began to mercilessly attack all the people who followed, in a truly crude generalization, the communist ideology. One day—I don't remember exactly—I was sick in bed, and a colleague came to tell me that something had occurred that I suspected for a long time would happen. (We were a union, very democratic, a union that certainly didn't respond to the Peronist party, a union that was very well known in the field of culture in Argentina.) It came about that the AAA had left a note in the bathroom of a bar, threatening us with death if we didn't leave the country in forty-eight hours. This happened in 1974, in September 1974.

Hector Alterio, Horacio Guaraní, Nacha Guevara, Norman Brisky, and myself were included in this threat. Previously, I had received a sort of warning on May 1 of that year. At that time, as was the custom, along with all the other declarations in the newspapers from the labor unions, ours appeared as well. And I remember that the AAA punctured my tires, poured acid all over my car, the gas tank, everything. And they left me a newspaper clipping on the windshield of my car from the newspaper *Clarín*, with our declaration as a warning.

We were against the repression's censorship, et cetera, et cetera; at that time there was a lot of censorship. It's been a long fight on the part of the actors' association for many decades. In general, people who work in the field of culture, historically, have not been very docile toward dictatorships. The field of culture in Argentina appeared during dictatorships that went on for many years, from 1930 until 1983, with brief pauses of democracy, and even during these brief pauses of democracy, there were certain limits on freedom of expression. It was a very difficult bone for the authoritarian governments to chew on. Therefore, culture was always under suspicion. In this case, it was very obvious. During the time of the AAA, the people working in culture demonstrated their opposition, and during the military dictatorship all the more so.

I received a written threat, but I really can't remember if it was in 1975 when I returned or before. The threat made its way to the Actor's Association. It was a hollowed-out stick of dynamite, written on both sides warning me that my family and I were in danger. It's certain that I was the recipient of this threat as much as Guaraní and Nacha and Brisky. I tried to stay in the country, to resist, but it really was impossible. I couldn't act in the theater, as you can well imagine. My life at home became so insupportable that three or four days afterward, we left the country.

The day after I received this death threat, there was a meeting in one of the headquarters of the Actor's Association in Viamonte street. More than four hundred or five hundred people came to denounce the death threats. At the same time that we were at this meeting, the AAA carried out quite a spectacular operation in a nearby neighborhood. They blockaded the street with cars, one in the opening of one street, one in the opening of the other. The brother of ex-President Frondizi, Silvio Frondizi, was living in the middle of the block. They menaced the people who looked out from their balconies. They took out Frondizi and his son-in-law, and they killed both of them. They took them away in a car with such brutal impunity. A few hours afterward, they appeared, dead.

They blockaded a street at three o'clock in the afternoon! They cut off an entire street! They waited for him there and took him away.

Frondizi was very important. He was a very important intellectual, a scientist. And they took him. Soon afterward, I left.

I went to Mexico, not for an artistic or political reason, but simply because I had a friend in Mexico who was going to accept me in his house. And I stayed there for ten months. And I returned. I tell you, it doesn't have to do with your work, but the sensation of exile is pretty indescribable. It's difficult to be able to explain the sensation of impotence, of anguish, that this creates. I was full of anguish in Mexico. We went to buy the newspapers every day, and almost every day there were death notices, results of terrorism or the AAA. But deaths every day. Two, one, six, twelve. It was something brutal. We were all crazy, at least I was, from anguish. And when two days went by when there wasn't any news of deaths, of political deaths, of political crimes, it began to give us the impression that things could get better. Well, anyway, I couldn't take any more. I had to return.

A few days after I got back, we had an interview with General Videla, who at this time was Jefe del Estado Mayor Conjunto. It is from him that I treasure a very important anecdote in my life.

Two colleagues, after the matter of the interview had been completed (a labor issue, concerning the debt that the television channels had with the actors, et cetera) asked him about the possibilities of my working. "A friend of ours has just gotten back from Mexico; he had been threatened. Do you think that he can work or not?" And Videla said, "I'm not going to speak about this because I'm involved in this issue, Mr. Brandoni, I'd rather not give my opinion." And I said, "No, give your opinion. Give your opinion, General. It will be helpful." He said, "No, because I don't agree with you." And I, "What do you think?" "The AAA threatened me as well," Videla said, "and I stuck it out here, while you left the country."

Their general, the commander of the Armed Forces, of the three Armed Forces, compared himself with me, an actor who had been threatened, and Videla, really macho, says, "I stuck it out while you left."

Later, July 9, 1976, with the dictatorship firmly planted in Argentina, my wife and I were kidnapped by a para-police unit, which afterward we found out was that of Aníbal Gordon. Aníbal Gordon was an AAA man who had an operational group that included Guglielminetti, and they took us to a clandestine detention center that was called Automóviles Orletti. There we were for several hours in this place where they had taken us. It seemed really big. There was a huge portrait of Hitler. There were Nazi symbols, et cetera. Aníbal Gordon asserted his claim to the AAA. He told me, "You were threatened by the AAA. We are the AAA. We told you to leave the country. You left, but you came back. You shit on us. Now we're going to shit on you."

Afterward, years later, I found out why we were able to get out of this. Gordon was held prisoner during the democratic government of Alfonsin. I found out from a lawyer from CELS, Mignone's Center for Legal Studies, that a military officer had saved us. This lawyer asked if we had a relative in the military, and we said no. "But it has to be. A relative."

"I don't have a relative in the military."

"A friend in the military?"

"I don't have a friend in the military. Neither does my wife." Then, I thought, the only soldier that I knew apart from my military service—and I never saw anyone from there again—was called Cordeta. General Cordeta. This lawyer told me that it was he. It was Cordeta. He had died a few years before. He had been chief of the Federal Police. He had brought a case before the tribunal, the only case in which a group of terrorists had been tried in accordance with the law and been put in jail. Let's say he was a very legalistic man. (He had many problems in the Federal Police.) He was a friend of a friend of mine, a colleague, and he was told the night they kidnapped us, this night he was told, and he must have pulled some sort of lever that he knew. Because of him, I'm telling you this. If not. . . .

They took us back to our house. Clearly, going and coming back, I was on the floor of one car, blindfolded, and my wife in another car. For much of the journey there as well as the return trip, they communicated by way of "motorola," with radios, and they had a code word, what we called a "holy standard," a code for this night—I think it was called "green frog," by which the entire organization of police would leave the route free in order not to have any interference. This really shocked me. Let's say, it was a confirmation that the security forces participated in this, at least by turning a blind eye. This guy that took me was a police officer from the intelligence services.

They had been part of the AAA. Ideologically, they were part of the AAA, but they didn't work for the AAA. Afterward, it was disbanded, let's say, once López Rega was forced to leave in September or October 1975. It appeared that by 1976—July 9, 1976—the AAA as an organization was shut down. It was the same people, but they worked for the terrorism of the state.

X

"El Angel"

It was a group in the hospital that was defined politically, that's for sure. We worked, we "militated," my wife as well, just like everyone else, everyone being active in Peronism.

This is how Raúl, or "el Angel" as he is known to his old friends, describes the generation of doctors at the Children's Hospital in Córdoba in the early 1970s. He, as well as many of the other young pediatricians at the time, was a follower of Peronism, that mystical political movement that seemed, like Saint Paul, to be all things to all people, promising socialism to the left, a buffer against Communism for the right, free trade for the industrialists, workers' rights to the unionists, stability for the center, nationalism to the nationalists, housing for the poor, and all the various mixtures in between that ex-president Juan

Domingo Perón could squeeze together through the force of his own personality. The doctors selected out of Perón's eclectic dogma his allusions to socialized medicine, and, disregarding the movement's more authoritarian overtones, saw in it the motor for change, not just for the Argentine health care system but for the entire society.

That was why in May 1973, when Hector Cámpora (Perón's hand-picked proxy, while Perón was still in exile) assumed the presidency of the nation, the doctors in Córdoba decided it was time to act. The Argentine people had rid themselves of the latest military government and had opened their arms to Perón after eighteen years of exile. Why shouldn't the doctors follow this national lead and rid themselves of the director who had been installed during the last military government? The medical faculty mobilized and literally deposed the hospital's director. It was a time for change, they thought, a time for new beginnings.

El Angel recalls the part that he witnessed Julia play in this new generation. One year her senior, he oversaw the young doctor's work, corrected her, guided her, pushed her on. But their relationship was not based on what the older doctors of the hospital might have called "pure medicine." In their daily dealings they were much more than casual colleagues, enmeshed in the medical, political, and social drama of the hospital. They were, indeed, a change from what the hospital had seen before.

El Angel remembers having lunch with Julia at the hospital cafeteria each afternoon, discussing new programs for health care, rights for recent mothers, new medical techniques, and politics. He can still picture her at the political assemblies that they held at the hospital, wearing her light-blue jacket and blue jeans, and "chatitas" (a type of flats) that el Angel remembers distinctly were black, always black. For el Angel, Julia was

> a tremendously peaceful person. Hardly ever talked. I was a chatterbox. But she, she always listened. And I remember the meetings of the assemblies that we had. Her interventions were always brief, short, but very melodious. It wasn't like how we wasted

time talking. She was more concrete. But she never raised her voice. She spoke very softly. Very softly.

It was obvious that they had come from different backgrounds. Julia, the youngest child in a highly anti-Peronist household, had been shielded from any type of politics. Raúl, the son of a dedicated Communist, grew up using words such as "vanguard" and "proletariat" as part of his everyday vocabulary, and as he began to develop his own political notions, he strained forward in the traces of Marxism, as his father had trained him. But for both of these doctors, different in thinking before having entered the hospital, it was now Peronism that embodied their hopes and dreams, the inspiration for a better children's hospital and the possibility of a more just society.

El Angel recalls a day in late 1973 when there was a closed-door strike at the automobile factory situated a few hours away from the Children's Hospital in Córdoba. It was a type of sit-in demonstration, produced by a split in the union's right-wing management and the decidedly left-wing workers. In a show of solidarity, el Angel and several other Peronist doctors from the hospital had come to cheer on the striking workers. "The people outside the factory were demonstrating in the doorway of the factory in support of the workers inside," el Angel says. "It was there that I saw Julia Andrea."

El Angel was surprised to see Julia there. They had talked about politics before, but they had never participated in a demonstration together, and he didn't know why she had come alone. When the speeches were over and the crowd thinned, they stayed and chatted for a while. El Angel said to Julia, "If you want, let's go. I have a car, and I can drop you off at Córdoba City." She replied, "No. I won't go. I'm going to stay here in the doorway, because my brother's inside." She was referring to Luis Ignacio, her oldest brother, a union organizer in the factory and one of the main leaders in the protest. The day remains fixed in el Angel's mind as an example of Julia's devotion to her brother and further illustrates why so many of Julia's friends believe that her close relationship with Luis Ignacio ultimately led to her disappearance.

On June 20, 1973, the Peronist dream ended. It is a date el Angel and most of his generation remember well, painfully and clearly, and if the comparison can be made, it was Argentina's Pearl Harbor. Juan Domingo Perón was scheduled to arrive at Ezeiza international airport, heralding the return of Peronism after eighteen years of exile and the beginning of what appeared to be the new Argentina.

Hundreds of thousands of supporters, militants, and lookers-on drove, took buses, hitchhiked, and walked to the airport, forming a long and expectant trail winding its way north and out of Buenos Aires. It was a mélange of those who were old enough to remember Perón from the postwar golden years as well as those who had been born after his exile, having been taught in secret by their parents to love, or having had the notion drilled into their heads by the public schools to despise, this enigmatic and aging dictator. They rose together to march upon the airport, to catch their first glimpse of Perón after all these years.

What they didn't know was that several right-wing death squads had been placed in charge of airport security and had ringed the perimeter with irregulars, armed and ready for a deadly confrontation with the left.

There, among the mass, hopeful, as were so many of the people there and equally unaware of the danger, was el Angel accompanied by his wife, then seven months pregnant. El Angel did not see Julia at the march, but he found out later that she had been there, as back at the hospital they breathlessly recounted the day's events. Julia marched with her fellow Peronists, accompanying her brother along the way to the balcony where Perón was to give his return speech: All the anticipation of a generation. The hope for change. Then, suddenly, everything went terribly wrong.

There has never been an official explanation for the events at Ezeiza, nor a trial of those assumed responsible. All that is known for certain is that one group opened fire, perhaps from the trees ringing the area, and another group, possibly from nearby the balcony, responded. Soon the whole scene was reduced to a bloody chaos of firing and responding to fire. Although el Angel is quick to say that the weight of blame lies with the right-wing groups, it cannot be denied that certain leftist groups, including the notorious Montoneros, had brought along their guns as well. In the confusion, members of the same faction reportedly began firing at each other, and the mass of civilians who had come to see Perón, from the right, center, and left, fell against each other, random targets of gunmen.

A man standing next to el Angel suddenly fell to the ground, downed by a rifle shot. El Angel grabbed his startled wife by the hand and started running through the crazed crowd, looking for some sort of shelter. He came across an ambulance that had been provided by the Unión Obrera Metalúrgica (Union of Steel Workers), one of the various groups that had participated in the march. He threw open the door, hoping to hide himself and his wife inside. There was, however, little space inside the ambulance, as it was filled with machine guns and other weapons. El Angel grabbed his wife again and hurried on.

The events of June 20, 1973, were taken as proof by the left and the right wings alike that no quarter should be given to their respective enemies, and that it would be through armed struggle alone that victory would be attained or lost. The bodies spread across Ezeiza that day became the symbol of Argentina's short-lived hope for democracy, and Ezeiza marked the beginning of the long and twisting road to leftist terrorism and right-wing reprisal. The violent right had finally shown its face in the Alianza Anticomunista Argentina (Argentine Anti-Communist Alliance or AAA), and the violent left, already established in the early 1970s, in the Montoneros and the Ejército Revolucionario Popular (People's Revolutionary Army). They all dug in for the long fight ahead.

Each day as he drove to work, the future darkened for el Angel, as he saw an increasing number of mutilated bodies strewn by the side of the road. Toward the end of 1974 the AAA was responsible for the murder of nearly seventy people: suspected terrorists, leftists, intellectuals, and union leaders. Perón could not trouble himself to put a stop to it. Rather, he reaped the benefits of ridding his country of the more troublesome sectors of Peronism, thereby stabilizing his government. In his Labor Day speech of May 1974, Perón characterized his once-faithful disciples, the Peronist Youth and the Montoneros, as "callow and stupid." It was clear that their dream was over.

In August 1974, fearing for his life and that of his wife, el Angel decided to leave Córdoba for the southern province of Chubut, away from the politics of the hospital and the politics of murder. Tired and disillusioned, he established himself as the only pediatrician in a small rural clinic.

On his first day at the southern outpost, he introduced himself to his new colleagues as Raúl (his baptismal name), leaving behind his old nickname in Córdoba, along with the personality that came with it. Once a political activist, a militant Peronist, el Angel became Raúl, the respected professional, part of the budding southern bourgeoisie. He worked overtime in the hospital, saved his money, bought a new house, and cut almost every tie that he had to Córdoba and to the past. He reflects:

> I have a friend who was taken prisoner, and when he was released, he said to me, "I was lucky that they 'sucked me in' because inside the prison I could conserve my ideas. You remained free, and they sucked the ideas out of you."

Raúl says this with a laugh, but then he pauses for a moment and there is a deep silence. He had closed an important door in his life, and he never saw Julia alive again.

It was only through talking to a man who used to sell vegetables in his old neighborhood that Raúl found out Julia's brother had been kidnapped, and it was two years after the fact when the news reached him that Julia had also disappeared.

As the years passed, Raúl became a different person, more careful and more secretive, but the shadows of his early militancy continued to haunt him. The house he kept in Córdoba was sacked on a number of occasions by unknown persons while he was in Chubut. He recognized this was the work of the same kind of group that had terrorized the doctors before, that had broken into Julia's house in 1975, and that had killed several of his colleagues. He took this as a vivid warning to stay clear of the hospital, and so he returned only once each year to visit relatives, but he never went back to see his old friends. One year, however, Raúl did go see his friends, those who were left. He recounts:

> I went to see my old boss, Francisco, and when he saw me, he put his arms around me and cried because they had said that I had died. I had come here to Chubut, and I didn't go any more to the hospital. I disappeared from my place where everyone knew me.

Raúl still works in the hospital in Chubut. He has a new car and a large family and is well known in the village for his expertise in assisting childbirth. Although he still returns to Córdoba each year to visit relatives, he seldom goes back to the hospital. When he does, he cannot enter the building without being overwhelmed by the past. As he walks down the front entrance corridor, he sees a young doctor, "militant" and inspired, striding off to save a life or to give a speech in this place of camaraderie and change. Then this brief vision fades, and he sees an older doctor, one less sure of his future and of his generation. He does not belong there any more, a visitor from out of town in a place out of touch with the past and the events that happened there long ago.

> I feel badly when I'm in the hospital because of the people I remember who were murdered. When I go to the hospital, I can't remove the image from inside of me. I feel, I don't know, a sensation of sadness and nostalgia. When I enter the hospital, I want to leave. When I'm outside, I want to go inside. I see the people, so far removed from everything that happened. There isn't one ward that contains their names, a library that bears their names. We studied a lot in the library. In the room where they worked so much, number fifteen, we could make a memorial because it was Julia Andrea's consultary. No one cares enough to do this. Absolutely no one. I believe that it's a necessity to wipe the memory from one's mind.

Many people who work at the hospital now were not there during the early 1970s, the turbulent years of semidictatorship and the beginning of complete tyranny. They are unaware of the history that lies dormant in the halls and wards and winding passageways, of other doctors, long ago, who cared and worked and fought for human rights and were killed for it. There are some in the hospital, however, who lived through those dangerous and brilliant times, who once remembered it all so vividly, but who now choose to push back the memories and go on. Raúl says that this is part of human nature, to change one's colors, to swallow lies, and to go on. And perhaps, he says, changing colors is not the same as forgetting. Perhaps it's just a defense mechanism that we all need in order to survive.

Just as el Angel once needed to disappear, once needed to be absorbed into the security of that anonymous southern village, Raúl now needs to talk about Julia and about all of the people who were once a part of his life and then were taken away from him:

> I speak like this because one has the necessity of speaking. To have someone in front of you that appreciates the subject, is very rare. The subject is taboo. . . . But I believe that Julia's life is worth a lot for history. I believe it's important not to let the names fall into oblivion. I believe that you always have to retrieve it as our national heritage. At best, they died so that we could continue to live, no?

General Heriberto Justo Auel

Retired from the Argentine Army; active during el
Proceso de Reorganización Nacional; *current member*
of a think tank on military strategy.

We were involved in confronting a psycho-political aggression that sought to exchange the political system for a totalitarian-marxist system. It's very difficult to understand all of this because today we're looking at it after the fact. We were in the midst of disorder and confusion. Our answers in response to this model of aggression were absurd. The president of the Republic decreed the *aniquilamiento* of an enemy that didn't have a front. There wasn't anywhere that this extermination could be accomplished on the battlefield. After the initial operations, such as operation Independencia Tucumán, this war was carried to the large cities.

The enemy had taken the initiative. When the initiative is taken, the freedom of action is taken. These centers of violence had to be eliminated somehow. And this new strategy was in the hands of many people. There was a dispersion of the unified command; there wasn't any strategy. There wasn't a defined concept of operation, and grave errors were committed.

When they were in the mountains, the enemy wore a uniform and practiced the theory of the *foco*, of power bases in the countryside, basing themselves on the ideas of Che Guevara and the translation of ideas from Mao Tse-tung. When they saw they didn't have the support of the people from the Argentine countryside they moved to the city. In the city they didn't use flags, distinctive uniforms. Instead, they normally used disguises. They dressed up like women, even pregnant women, with babies in baby carriages that were really dolls. And in the baby carriages, there was normally a bomb that was tossed into a supermarket or at the door of some barracks, and we suffered the death of a lot of people as a result of this. Above all, this situation brought desperation because when this type of aggression and conflict occurs, without having taken precautions, the state reacts late, and it makes mistakes. We didn't have a strategy, we didn't have planning. And the desperation changed the political system that was already in decline.

It is difficult to explain the subject of the detention camps. Why? Because the enemy established a model of aggression that is evasive, that lies outside of the rules of war. The Geneva Convention doesn't accept this model as being aggression. Therefore, this put us in the position of using the law of the Armed Forces that didn't have judicial support. Because of this, afterward, the military commanders, who operated against this enemy and made decisions in terms of a presidential decree that called for the extermination of this enemy, were all judged by the penal justice code. That is to say, a problem that was initially political, and not judicial, was made judicial.

This was a drama of misunderstanding, of improvisations, of a lack of professionalism, deep analysis, and knowledge of contemporary conflict. This was a serious problem. The type of terrorism that the

U.S. had was a spin-off of a consumer society. Here, no. Here, this terrorism was a product of political subversion that was attempting to change the system. It's quite distinct. That is why, when the people from the north come here to analyze us, with mistaken criteria, it's a conversation with diverse parameters, and there's a total lack of communication.

I'm going to repeat myself. Rules of war are found in the laws of war. They are in the Geneva Convention. The enemy went beyond the Geneva Convention. That was their strong point. That was, let's say, the slot by which they filtered through and brought about the confusion. The state should have reacted, giving specific judicial reasoning against the aggression of this type of model. And it didn't do it. We were left with the old system of justice that looked after public security but not to the security of the state. The security of the state is in the hands of the defense, and the defense has, for its legal regulations, the Geneva Convention. But the Geneva Convention doesn't accept this model of aggression.

Not only did the enemy hide in jungle foliage, like in Vietnam, but they also hid in the cement "foliage" of the large cities and the "foliage" of the people who live in these big cities, camouflaging themselves there as citizens, but they were armed, and they produced this violence that made society desperate. People died as they were leaving their houses because a car passed by and the guerrillas threw a grenade.

From a balcony, we didn't know from where, a single rifle shot struck a man right outside his house, as he was saying goodbye to his family. That happened to a friend of mine. And we never knew who killed him. It was a bullet that came from some place. It was never known from where. This created desperation. The same that you think with respect to the drama that you lived through in Vietnam. Exactly the same. When the enemy perceives that we have a state in tatters, when we have military leaders who are not professionals and politicians who have not studied the theory of contemporary conflict—nor does it matter to them—then the enemy finds that they can take the initiative, have the freedom of action, and make the centers of cities virtual traps.

Human rights and political rights are the values of our political culture, not the political culture of the enemy. But we appropriate political rights and human rights. That is to say, the strategic objective the enemy pursued in this phase of the campaign developed in order to take the power from the state; they pursued this issue in order to retain as their objective the destruction of the Armed Forces as well as of the state of human rights, and they raised as their own banner the same human rights that were our own, from the American Revolution.

Here, today, we can legitimize the actions. I believe that they are legitimized, considering what the objective was. We didn't have an alternative because we didn't have a state. There had to be an improvisation, and in the improvisation all sorts of errors were committed.

No, it's not "well done." I'm recognizing that there was an enormous quantity of errors because of the improvisation. Because we were surprised. The only way to do things well and not destroy our own values is to take precautions from the beginning.

The Armed Forces were left outside, estranged from the state, from the nation. And this worsened when Alfonsín put on trial—a political act—the military, as responsible for genocide. What is responsible for genocide is the Argentine nation, which lacked a state, which lacked professionalism in the Armed Forces, which lived through a structural crisis that was felt for many years. It's the entire group together that's guilty for what went on.

X I

Ana María

Ana María doesn't know the date on which they kidnapped her. It was either March 17 or 18, 1977. After all these years, she can't remember the date, although she remembers the day clearly enough, as if it happened yesterday.

She had just awakened. Her father was downstairs having breakfast and drinking mate. She remembers how he used to affectionately call her "museum rat" because she spent most of her time at the university in Buenos Aires, lost among the books and the bones, studying anthropology. At twenty-two years old, she was an aspiring anthropologist with three years left to go before she graduated. Her future seemed to be settled. Graduation, a career, marriage, perhaps a family. And then came the knock on the door. Ana María recalls:

> They knocked on the door, really softly, at nine o'clock in the morning. My father said to me, "It's probably your mother who's

coming back from the bank." (My mother had gone to do an errand at the bank.) And the door opened and, vroom, in came fifteen people, armed to the teeth.

Most of the men were quite young, the youngest probably no more than seventeen. They were dressed in civilian clothes, although it was obvious that they were part of a military group. The leader, the oldest in the group, was called *comandante* by the rest. He immediately began interrogating Ana María concerning her sister's boyfriend whom they or another of the many paramilitary groups had kidnapped a few days earlier.

As they bombarded her with questions, Ana María's mind went back to the conversation that she had had with her sister two days before. "I'm leaving. I'm leaving," her sister had said. "Come with me to the countryside." "Look, I'm not going, because in the end you're going to get caught," Ana María said. Her sister left for the country in tears, leaving Ana María upset but unconvinced that she was in any danger. Her sister's boyfriend had been part of the Juventud Peronista Universitaria (University Peronist Youth) and had obviously been involved in something. It was "natural," then, that he should be taken and that they would come looking for her sister.

> Without any doubt they came looking for my sister because after being inside, that is, after they took me away, I learned that they had tortured her boyfriend in a frightening way, and, well, during the torture he gave up my sister's name.

But Ana María had nothing to be afraid of, or so she thought at the time. She hadn't done anything wrong. In fact, she hadn't done anything, anything that might even have been misconstrued as being dangerous. She wasn't politically active. She didn't belong to a political movement, and as for being a militant, she hardly knew which groups were which. She studied, and that was all.

Unfortunately for Ana María, however, the paramilitary group did not put as much faith in Ana María's innocence as Ana María did. If her sister could not be found, then they would take Ana María as proxy. As she was still in her nightgown, they let her change clothes in the bathroom. Looking through the bathroom window, she could see the street had been completely cut off, two cars, men carrying machine guns. It looked like something out of the movies. It didn't seem possible that all of this had been done for her. Two men towered on either side of her as they bundled her out the door. The handcuffs they had put on her were almost falling off because her wrists were so thin. She saw the people staring at her, those who had come out to see what all the noise was about, and Ana María thought, "What kind of a person will the neighbors think I am?" She left her father stunned, still drinking mate in the kitchen.

When they put me in the car (that's where they threw me) they put a bag over my head, *una capucha*. The journey began, and they asked me, "*Nombre de guerra!* What is your *nombre de guerra?*"
"What *nombre de guerra?*"
"Well, how do you call yourself?"
"Ana María. I'm Ana María."

Ana María had just become one of the disappeared.

Soon the car stopped, and Ana María heard some of the men shouting as they jumped out of the car to chase a woman they thought they had recognized. Ana María heard the woman screaming as they tried to take her. Tilting her head back a bit, Ana María could just make out under her bag the brickwork of a church she recognized, and she realized that she was only a few blocks away from her house. The men came back without the woman, saying, "No, no. We were confused. We were confused." They continued on to the local police station

and that's where the dance began. They covered me up, put a really tight blindfold on me, put me in a corner. It's like they forgot about me for a while because they were doing something, torturing someone, some guy. I listened to voices. I only listened to voices. A woman participated in the torturing, who, later I found out, was a Montonero. Afterwards, it was said that she had been killed as well. People collaborated, that's for sure, in order to get out of being tortured, or whatever. . . .

Ana María was thrown on a mattress, and a soldier approached her. He said, "Think, think, think . . . or if not, if you don't talk, I can do this to you," referring to the screams that Ana María heard. She was then thrown together with a woman whom she would later learn was called Amanda. That night, Ana María escaped further punishment, left to huddle in the darkness. But Amanda was not to be as fortunate; as she recounted from exile while in Spain:

> They tied my ankles and wrists to a chair, they wrapped a piece of plastic over my face that stopped me from breathing. After a while of interrogation, they took me to another room where a man who was called *el coronel* talked to me, telling me that I should give them the information or, if not, they would continue to beat me. They put the blindfold on me again, and brought me to the room I was in before; they tied me to a chair, wrapped a piece of plastic over my face again and interrogated me concerning my political affiliation, until, because of my convulsions—due to the fact that I wasn't able to breathe—I fell over with the chair.

That night, the soldiers moved both women by car, Amanda in the trunk and Ana María on the floor. They made their way to a detention center called Arana, which was better known by its occupants as "the little camp" or "the house of torture." All the new prisoners were made to sit in a hall, a waiting room for torture. Ana María heard voices, people screaming, soldiers shouting, but she still couldn't see anything. As Ana María waited in the hallway, terrified, it was again Amanda who received the worst of what the soldiers had to offer. Amanda relates how

> they took off my clothes, made me lie down over a mattress on the floor; they tied my ankles and wrists to the framework that was underneath the mattress and began to apply electricity to me, over my entire body, and at the same time, they covered my face with a pillow. At one point, they told me that they had detained

my mother in the room next door and that I would hear her screams when they started to interrogate her if I continued not to talk.

Then the soldiers moved Ana María to the torture room, tied her down on the mattress in order to apply *la picana*, or electric current. They asked her about her sister's whereabouts. "I don't know. I don't know," she said. "But you have to know," was the response. "I don't know," she cried. Then they asked her about students from the anthropology school, if she knew any people in the guerrilla movements. Ana María was thoroughly confused. She didn't even know how to begin answering their questions. She again replied that she didn't know, that she didn't know anyone who was a guerrilla. The interrogators were satisfied with this for the moment, and they left Ana María without applying the prod, telling her, "We'll call you again."

She was put into a holding cell with people she assumed were other prisoners, although she couldn't see anything. They were blindfolded and tied, not allowed to talk. They could only sit on the floor and listen to the sound of people being tortured on the other side of the wall and the sounds of the newly arriving. It was hot, Ana María remembers, "a complete hell." Mosquitoes swarmed around them in the darkness. A guard came in once and sprayed insecticide over them, an unexpected act of mercy. "It was like a great insanity, a generalized insanity. I remember I thought that I was inside an insane asylum." But amid the madness, there was Julia:

> We were seven there. And this night is where I remember that I trembled like a leaf, trembled, and I couldn't stop. And I remember that someone touched me, and it was Julia. It's something unbelievable to meet someone that gives you a little bit of affection, without restraint. That's a little bit of the image I have of her.

Relating the experience in the light of day, calmly, able to pause, able to go on again, Ana María's contact with Julia seems brief, she says, perhaps too brief to be important. But in the darkness of that little cell, among the mosquitoes and the blood, the pain, the screams, Julia's touch was the only reference point that Ana María had for humanity. The women prisoners were like broken things, washed up on the beach, but for one moment the wave of barbarity receded and there was an unseen hand, proving to Ana María that someone still cared. It was enough for her to make it through the night.

Ana María remembers Amanda complaining about some wounds that she had on her legs. (The day Amanda had been taken, she had fallen down in the street, trying to run away. During the torture sessions the soldiers had applied electric shocks to her wounds.) But there was almost no other communication, no sounds from the women, except groans and weeping:

> With Julia, that's the only contact I had with her. I felt that she was very calm, no? After, we said a few words. That is to say, I found out that she was pregnant, that she was a doctor, but nothing more. We hardly ever talked. You couldn't talk.

The only record of contact between Amanda and Julia is similar to Ana María's brief description of Julia given in Amanda's testimony, in which she recalls that Julia was two months pregnant, that she worked just outside of Buenos Aires, that she needed to take her medication for her heart condition but that the guards never gave it to her. Finally, Amanda mentions that the soldiers questioned Julia concerning people who worked in popular medicine. Ana María and Amanda spent four days in Arana before being transferred to La Comisaría Quinta on March 22. They never saw Julia again.

Some time after Julia was taken away, a soldier appeared at Ana María's cell and transferred her to another holding area. He asked her if she was scared, and she said, "Yes."

> "You're not going to have any problems," he replied. And they took me to a place that looked like (I didn't see anything. I could hear noises.) an office, and you could hear typewriters. There was a room, and he asked me if I had taken a bath.

"Yes, one time."

"Well, here you can take a bath."

He was really well-mannered. He said to me, "Look, I voted for you to be freed."

In reality, the hand was coming, whatever he wanted—he wanted to have sexual relations with me. This was really common. For them, it's something that you don't choose. You don't do anything.

Ana María didn't know if she was ever going to be freed. She had no way of knowing. But she knew that she couldn't accept what he was offering her, better treatment, freedom, if she had sex with him. She struggled against him as he tried to convince her, saying that he was an official in the army, an important man in the torture center, that it would be good for her.

And I said, "Look, I don't like having relations with someone I don't know." And all of this was very absurd, but very clear. And suddenly, he became violent and said, "Well, if I want, I can do whatever I want with you." I was naked, there was a bed, and I thought this is a really big guy, and I was blindfolded. And he said to me, "Listen to me. . . . What is this! You've never been with a man before?" I said, "No, I've never been with a man." "Ah," he says, "But please, you should have told me before." And he said, "Well, okay, get dressed."

Through some bizarre code of honor that permitted this soldier to rape only women who were not virgins, Ana María was saved from yet another humiliation. She got dressed and was taken again by car to another place. She was left standing on a street corner, told not to take off her blindfold until she could no longer hear the sound of the car that had taken her. When she took off her blindfold, she saw that she was two blocks from her house. It was two o'clock in the morning, as Ana María ran towards her house in desperation. She rang the bell, and her parents came to the door, looking as if they had aged one hundred years.

Up until the arrival of democracy in 1983—and even today, Ana
María says—many Argentines have said that the prison centers, the
disappearances, rapes, murders, were pure leftist fantasy, held-over
terrorist ideology, part of a campaign to discredit Argentina's military.
And the disappeared? Well, if they did exist at all, they were permitted
to escape, and are now sipping piña coladas in la Habana or working
as waiters in Berlin or, worse still, among Argentine society, perhaps
in the far northern provinces, living under assumed names and planning their next acts of terrorism. As for Ana María, who are the disappeared? Who is Julia?

> I consider them to be ghosts. I felt like a ghost, too, because I
> had lived through it all, and when I returned to reality, let's say
> this reality, the reality of those on the outside, I didn't know what
> to do with myself. Because I saw that I couldn't talk. You can only
> tell certain people, "You know, I was disappeared." It had to be
> someone that you trusted a lot. I didn't have the space. I closed
> myself off a lot, I closed myself off a lot. I went to work. I went
> home. I didn't have friends because I was very afraid. Because of
> that you kept it, kept it lodged inside, for many years.

No longer the twenty-two-year-old anthropology student, Ana
María lives in the outskirts of Buenos Aires, teaching weaving to ele-
mentary school students. She gave up anthropology years ago out of
fear and out of "anti-nostalgia" for the university. In one of those
many years after she was released, she found someone to whom she
could tell her story, married him, had a child, and later separated. At
last she is beginning to find her space in her weaving, as she tries to
express the many emotions and truths that were forbidden her for so
many years. Through the patterns, angles, and designs, one imagines
her trying to weave a way, a way to explain what it was like to be
disappeared:

> I ran from the place where they could take me, but this story of
> fear is a story that has been latent for many years, of police cars,
> if they stop, if they don't stop. We lived with this for a long time.

Dr. Luis Gabriel Moreno Ocampo

Prosecuting attorney in the trial of the military junta;
educator; specialist in the field of corporate and goverment
corruption; cofounder of citizen's action committee, Poder
Ciudadano (Citizen Power).

The law established that the military should be tried under military jurisdiction. There are some people who say that these were military crimes and not crimes that should be tried in civilian court. So, what the government of Alfonsín did was to modify the procedure, establishing that the military tribunals could appeal to the equivalent of a circuit court. In general, Alfonsín's plan was for the military to try themselves, but in a debate in Congress a clause was formulated that said that if the military tribunals took a long time, the circuit court could withdraw the case and take over the case and try it directly like a normal trial. In reality, this is what happened.

The federal court of appeals withdrew the case, and a panel of six judges tried it as if it were a normal court acting in a normal trial. The change was that in Argentina there was an investigatory closed procedure. On the other hand, the military code provides for summary oral trials. So by way of a reform of the military court, an oral trial was permitted. This was the first oral trial that was ever handled in the Argentine federal system. This had an enormous impact, because, after five months of hearings, after the preparation for the trial, every day there were fifteen, twenty witnesses each day. There were 830 witnesses. This had a very large impact.

When I arrived at the public prosecutor's office, we began to take a look. The problem was, how could we accuse those in charge of actions they had not personally committed? We could accuse them of having killed thirty thousand people, but when could a trial concerning thirty thousand people ever end? We didn't have proof for the thirty thousand individuals. So what we did was select a very few cases that were the strongest. Moreover, [we chose] those cases that proved the different armed forces, the Air Force, the Army, the Navy, responsible. Furthermore, Alfonsín, as head of the Armed Forces, according to the military code, had to issue a decree in order to accuse a general. Therefore, Alfonsín issued a decree naming the nine leaders of the military juntas, in his capacity as chief of the military. Those who had been president of the juntas were judged. From 1976–1978, afterward, 1978–1981, and 1981–1982. We had to find cases that were very strong, cases that pointed to the involvement of the different armed forces. The thesis of the prosecutor general's office was that the Junta acted as the only organ of command.

It doesn't matter that there wasn't a law of *Obediencia Debida*. We were attributing the responsibility for having ordered and having planned these acts, like when the leader of a gang is punished for having planned a bank robbery. The leader didn't rob the bank, but his gang members did. It was the same here. The soldiers had done things because their bosses had ordered them to. That was our thesis.

The most severe repression was during 1976–1980. Therefore, the judges considered the leaders in 1981–1982 as not having violated human rights in a massive way. So they absolved the last four commanders of the Air Force, the Navy, the Army. There were four people absolved. And among the condemned they handed down very different punishments because they considered that each armed force acted independently. We said that they were at least accomplices, but well. . . .

It was all a very complex process in which there were trials for five months so that the people saw what was going on in Argentina; it had a very astounding impact. My mother is the daughter of a general. And my mother lived in the same area as the presidential house in Olivos. So, for my mother, Videla was a wonderful person. I said, well, we'll start with my mother, proving that they're guilty, and that's how we'll change Argentina, because my feeling was that we had two fronts: We had to win the trial in court, and we had to win the trial in the public opinion.

And the trial had just that, a great impact on public opinion. Two weeks into the trial, after two weeks of listening to testimonies of the horrors, my mother was convinced.

In reality, this was about a strategy of operations against guerrillas that the Argentines learned from the French in Algeria. Three colonels from the French army that had operated in Algeria came to Argentina at the beginning of the sixties and showed how to divide the country into quadrants so that there were small sectors with very clear heads. And this is what Argentina did. A system was set up, the country was divided into zones and sub-zones, areas and sub-areas, with commanders whose roles were clear, so they all had controlled territory. Overall, this is where they operated, the chiefs of the zones and subzones, not the chiefs of the repression. And this was what we had to prove to demonstrate personal responsibility in a court of law. The military had orders that established jurisdiction along the chain of command. No order said that they should torture and kill people.

All of them recognized that they were heads of the zones, all of them in the Armed Forces recognized that there were people who kidnapped in these places, that the victims were transported by military trucks; in others, by the police, by groups that depended on the Army; where they tortured; afterward they put the victims in airplanes and threw them into the ocean. All of this, the only way that this could happen, was if it were planned. From this starting point comes the inference that this happened by order of the commanders.

Well, because of this Videla was condemned. What happened was that there was a problem. Alfonsín promised trials, but afterward, the crime was so huge that the judges began to go beyond what Alfonsín thought the political system could allow. So the judges, after condemming Videla, said that they had to keep on trying those responsible in the zones, sub-zones, and sub-areas. Alfonsín didn't want this, and because of this, laws appeared that limited responsibility, first the law of *punto final*, in effect, a pardon. Because, if not, you'd have to put thousands of people in jail, and he was very afraid that the military would mutiny.

This was the political conflict that occurred because there were two values at stake. What Alfonsín said was, "Look, we're pro-Justice, but what Justice wants is to place something very important, Democracy, in danger. After the law of *punto final*, there were about three hundred fifty people who were to be tried. After the law of *Obediencia Debida*, forty were left. There were seven who were condemned. They were pardoned in 1990. President Menem pardoned them, yes.

A difference with Nazi Germany is that in Nuremberg behind the judges there were the allied armies. And behind the accused there was no one. In Argentina, this is the paradox. Behind us there was only public opinion that demanded that this trial should be held. And the Army, the *Power*, the weapons, were behind the accused. Because of this, it explains the difficulty of the case, doesn't it?

I trusted in democracy. And for me, when they offered me the job of prosecuting attorney, I said, well, I'm going to accept. It's a risk, but I believe it's going to be better for democracy when it's consolidated. If it turns out badly, best not think about it twice, not think about it. If it turns out badly, I'm going to have to leave the country, I'm going to have to escape. I didn't have to think. If the military returns, I'm going to have to escape or they're going to kill me. That was my decision.

What is certain is that a massive crime of that magnitude can only be carried out by a government with hegemonic power. It's very difficult to do that with freedom of expression and with democracy. I believe that the trials served for many things, but basically to avoid personal vendettas because the government took on the problem. I believe that democracy in Argentina has been consolidated by the trials that were held. We live in countries in which the concept of law is quite different from that of Anglo-Saxon law. In the Anglo-Saxon model, the law is a way to protect the weak. In our model, which comes from medieval Spain, in all of Latin America, the law is a way for those that have power to control and punish their subjects. This is the model of medieval Spain, of Europe under the monarchies. In Brazil, there's a saying that is very well put that explains this: "For my friend, everything. For my enemy, the law." This model of law is a system of punishment. Because of this, the law is not an idea that has a relationship with our Latin American societies. The law is a way for those who have power to trouble us, nothing more. The trial of the juntas was the symbol, was a sign of change in this sense. It demonstrated that the law could become a system of protection, and that powerful people can fall under the law.

I believe that it was a step backward. It was a step backward, but it had to do with the political forces and the way in which these political issues were handled. But what happened is that in this society, let's say, when we were in the trials, we felt that, well, we're working, investigating things that look like what happened in Uganda. But after the trials, we're going to be living in Sweden. It's as if Argentina was becoming Sweden. I believe that the result of the trials and of the pardons has to do with a country that had mixtures, like that savagery in Uganda, as well as the possibility of having a very well-handled trial performed with democratic, clear rules like the Swedish model, and that a synthesis of such mixed and opposing forces is what happened in Argentina. There were trials, which was something amazing. The trials were limited. There were pardons afterward. It's difficult to say, but, well, it's like this—it was neither a complete fiasco nor was it as perfect as I had wished. That's how it is. That's how it is.

X I I

Silvina

On March 28, 1977, early in the morning, Silvina was transferred to the prison camp Arana. She had been kidnapped from her house the day before and had spent the night with other prisoners in a local police station in Buenos Aires. She sat in the same hall where Ana María, Amanda, and Julia had passed through a few days before. She was tied and blindfolded, like the rest. The guards read names of the prisoners from rosters, "just like in school," Silvina recalls. She had been a physics teacher at the Universidad de Buenos Aires and in her testimony before the National Commission on the Disappearance of People she later sadly recalled having recognized one of her former students among the victims there. She heard her husband's name called on the roster as well and assumed that he, too, had been captured. Silvina was seven months pregnant.

Precisely this same night of the twenty-seventh to the twenty-eighth, the early morning, they took me to be tortured. I was the last (later, I realized that I was the last). It seems that the torturers were tired for having tortured all night long. They asked me two or three questions, threatened me, and left me.

Soon after, probably that same day, although it was hard for her to tell, Silvina was pulled to her feet. Minutes had seemed hours. One counted the time passing by the sounds of the new prisoners arriving and the numbness brought about by the cold floor. Silvina was taken from where she was being held and led down a hallway. Doors opened and closed. Silvina was then taken to a room. She was filled with wild fear. Was she in front of a firing squad? Was there a pit of crocodiles?

I didn't know where I was. Everything was obscure, dark. There was nothing. There wasn't anything. I heard a voice that said, "Who are you?" And that was Julia Montesini, the first person I spoke with in the cell.

Silvina told Julia her name. As she slowly began to understand that she was in a holding cell, she also realized that there were three other women with her. But Silvina was still afraid:

At first, there was a lot of fear, a lot of fear of the unknown person whom you were talking to. A little less, when a person like Julia would say to you, "Don't worry now . . . if they brought you to the cell, that means they're not going to torture you any more." This was an important point. I can't assure you that it was she. But it doesn't matter.

At times, Silvina's memories of Julia blend with those of the other women. There were voices, hushed words, escaped phrases. Julia was a shadow and a voice, but little else. She could, in fact, have been a spy for all Silvina knew, trying to win Silvina's confidence, getting information out of her to trap and kill her later.

When the torture of one person stopped, between torturing that person and the next, we could talk. You couldn't listen to the

torture and be talking like little birds at the same time. When the
torture finished completely at night, then the women could begin
to talk to me, and the one I talked to the most was Julia, because
the others spoke very little. Then Julia began to tell me, "Well,
what's your name? Don't worry; we're all in the same boat; we've
been kidnapped; they torture here. . . ." I had realized that.

Silvina remembers Julia's voice as soothing, almost a balm against
what was going on. And she began to trust this voice, these few but
innocent-sounding words. "It was like a voice that didn't correspond
to the place, for being sweet, calm," she describes. Bit by bit, the
women began to tell each other who they were; where they had come
from; why, they thought, they had been captured. Names were important to them. If one of them were released, she could search out the
families of the rest and tell them where they were, that they were all
right, and not to worry.

It was over a year into the dictatorship, and still there was no public
talk of holding centers, concentration camps. Even the word *desaparecido* was not yet used to describe the large-scale terror that was under-
way, a terror daily felt but barely registered on the national conscience. Yes, it was obvious that people were being taken away, but
there was no sense of the scale of the operations, and it was always
easier to say the phrases that became famous later on, *Por algo será* or
En algo andará ("It must have been for a reason" that he was taken, or
"He must have been doing something" was easier than imagining that
the government had proclaimed its own secret war against all sectors
of Argentine society). As Silvina recounts:

> After the torture, after they tortured a woman that we heard,
> when we heard it all, the shouts, the questions, the answers, they
> opened the cell and put this woman in, recently tortured. This
> woman was called Elena. And after Elena came in, we spoke
> among the three of us. Let's say we were the ones who spoke
> the most. Elena was totally different from Julia. Elena was very
> energetic, with a lot of emphasis. On the other hand, Julia was
> very calm, very calm. Elena all tortured, her face destroyed, with

her lips bleeding. You could tell her mouth was destroyed by the way that she spoke; besides, the tongue, after the electricity goes through, it stays in your cheeks.

As Silvina recounts, "I didn't recognize Julia; we didn't see each other. I didn't know who she was or what she looked like." To Silvina, Julia was one of the several dark shapes, hunched shadows quietly breathing in the cramped room. This was Julia's cell—all of theirs. It was one meter by one meter eighty, shared by the five of them. Unable to lie down, they huddled together in the dark, seeking warmth at night from the anonymous shapes. Some just wanted to shut out the madness, trying to take some consolation from the fact that at least they were not alone. They slept or tried to sleep. The only bed was given to Silvina because of her advanced state of pregnancy.

Here were the Junta's terrorists, their dangerous revolutionaries: frightened women, blindfolded and bound in tiny rooms, several of them in different stages of pregnancy, some crying, others silent, trying to recover from the day's ration of electric shocks and beatings. In this one cell, as well as within the other unknown, uncounted cells peppered throughout Argentina, el Proceso's policies were being carried out. Defined March 24, 1976, in all of the Argentine newspapers, the ends the dictatorship sought were

> the complete observance of the moral and ethical principles of justice, of the integral organization of mankind, of respect for his rights and dignity; in this way, the Republic will achieve unity among Argentines and the total recuperation of the national self, convoked in a force that is common to all men and women that inhabit the earth without exclusion.

The lofty airs of "unity" and "total recuperation" of March 24 had degenerated into the terror that Julia and the rest of the women who waited with her in the darkness now faced. Here was el Proceso's equality, as each woman waited with equal anticipation to see who would be taken out next and shot.

Julia began to say a few words about her past life, how she was a doctor. She told Elena and Silvina that she was pregnant, that she had been taken at the clinic. She told Silvina how she had been taken to be tortured, but when they had stripped off her clothes, the doctor who monitored the session—to make sure the prisoner didn't die before she gave information—saw the scar from Julia's heart operation. The doctor said, "No, this one stays; this one's going to die" if she was tortured with electric shocks. "Leave her." Julia was threatened, interrogated, and returned to her cell. Silvina says:

> They didn't use *la picana* (cattle prod) on her, and, well, at this moment, the only thing that was important was *la picana* and *el submarino*. *El submarino* is when they put your head underwater. And the rest, just being there, wasn't considered torture. Today we see it in a different way.

Seven days without eating, their hands tied behind their backs, blindfolded, wasn't in itself considered torture. Indeed, it was quite the opposite. It was respite, asylum from what was happening to the less fortunate individuals strapped to the electric bed.

Silvina says that the women didn't think in terms of the "justice" or the "injustice" of their treatment. They accepted the fact that the dictatorship had taken them at face value, that they wanted information from them. Silvina says that she wasn't fearful for her own life, but for that of her unborn child. Two months from full term, she had heard stories of children being taken from their mothers, children who later ended up in those families of military and police officials who were unable to have children. Would this be her child's fate? She didn't know. Did she think that she was ever going to be freed?

> Of course. All of us. We never thought that we wouldn't. No one could think that. First, it took a lot to adapt yourself to the fact that you were in a clandestine concentration camp. Second, it took a lot to adapt yourself to the idea that this could go on for a long time. A day, two days, a week. Afterward, the hope was to be legalized, that you'd be taken to a legal jail. You thought they could kill some. What you couldn't understand was the delay.

Once tortured, once taken for information, it was the fear of immediate death. The days passed as months, and you met people who had been there a lot longer. One accepted this sickness, that this could be true. You didn't understand why so much time. If they were going to kill people, why keep them alive? And if they were going to let them live, why keep them hidden?

Julia asked herself the same questions. Why all of this secrecy if they were going to be freed? And if they weren't going to be freed, why keep them for such a long time? Silvina remembers that Julia was very worried about her brother, Luis Ignacio. She guarded hopes that he might be in the same detention center. She had no idea of the immensity of the disappearance network, that her brother could be held anywhere in Argentina. Less than a year had passed between her brother's disappearance and her own, and she hoped that he might be there, that he might still be alive; she hoped that she would pass him in the hallway as she was taken to the bathroom by one of the guards. The men were kept in a separate section of the concentration camp, away from the women. Was it Luis Ignacio who was screaming in the next room?

The most terrifying experience was waiting for the next *traslado*. Connecting the intricate route of detention centers to torture camps were the mass prisoner transfers, the *traslados*. But the final *traslado* was the one from which no one ever returned. One never knew if the next *traslado* was to another prison center—better, worse, legal, still clandestine—freedom, or death.

Friday, April 3, there was a transfer of most of the prisoners. Julia, Elena, and two other women, Mauricia and Estela, were escorted out of the cell and taken away. Silvina was left with a woman named Beba. The next day they finally came for Silvina, took her in a car to another place, supposedly another prison complex, but this time she was alone. Still blindfolded, she was escorted through a large door. Silvina could hear them opening a large grill. She was placed against a wall, and she said to herself, "They're going to shoot me." Then she heard the boots of the guard walking away, the door closed, and someone lowered her blindfold. She was in a large holding room with approximately sixteen women, among them, Elena and Julia.

The women were all there without blindfolds, in a much larger room, the first time they were able to see each other, to piece together the bits of conversations they had had with shadows, disconnected names, and put them to a face, a figure, a smile. Silvina describes the women as

> broken, dirty, uncombed, hurt, with wounds on the face, mouth, ears, with the clothes ripped. Imagine suddenly opening your eyes after a week of not seeing anything, opening your eyes and finding yourself in a leper colony. I had heard voices—Elena's voice, Julia's voice. It was impossible for the voices to correspond to the women because what was in front of me weren't women; they were human beings physically undone. I don't have an image of Julia because it was something overpowering, seeing all of them, to see sixteen or eighteen people destroyed is terrible. That's why I can't say, "This one's worse off" or "this one's Julia."

They had been reunited again, this time in the Comisaría Quinta in La Plata. Rules were different here, as Silvina soon found out. All in all, it was a concentration camp like Arana, but a vast improvement over the conditions where Silvina had just spent over a week. The women were allowed to keep their blindfolds lowered as long as the guards weren't close by, and their hands were left untied. This permitted them to wash their faces in the small sink they had in the room. And they were finally permitted to eat, broth served with two potatoes in it, which the guards served from a pot.

They kept watch, peeping through holes in the sheet metal that covered their cell. They would talk while the guards were gone, keeping their blindfolds lowered, ready to lift them in case they returned. They were hungry for information. As new prisoners came in, with new stories, they began to realize the incredible extent of the clandestine prison networks. Some women had been held for nine months. Others disappeared soon after arriving.

The phrase that has been most repeated by Julia's friends in regard to her kidnapping was that she did not "deserve" it, that she did not deserve to have been tortured and killed, that against the background of terrorism and revolution she stood out as being quite innocent. Silvina recounts that Julia fully understood the part she played in the concentration camps, and that she was under no illusion that innocence would serve as an aegis to save her life:

> There were other girls who asked themselves, who tortured themselves with asking "Why?"—who had, if you want to say it, less to do with it than Julia. Julia had it very clear, let's say, that she hadn't been part of the militancy but that her brother was a militant, and that this was enough for her to be there. It wasn't a surprise when you arrived there and realized the type of people who had been taken. There were people who were a lot less compromised than Julia. There, it was understood that it wasn't strange that she was there. Do you understand? There was one person there who was there for only having rented an apartment where a militant had lived before. Julia's case was not surprising. She didn't need to say that she understood the political situation, but by not asking stupid questions you realized who was who. There was a girl who spent the whole day crying because she didn't understand anything: "What am I doing here? Because I didn't do anything. I didn't do anything. What is this? They're going to believe me. They're going to believe me, they're going to let me go. They're going to understand me!" And Julia, Julia wasn't a militant in an armed group, but she realized the objective of the government was not only the militants of the armed groups but also anyone who could think.

Julia and several other prisoners were taken in a large transfer on April 21. Silvina and a few other women were left behind. On May 5, after her contractions became more and more severe, Silvina was taken by car to what she supposed at the time would be a clinic. While in route, Silvina gave birth to a girl. There was nothing to cut the umbilical cord with, so the woman named Natashia, who assisted the torturers, tied the cord, and they continued on. All the while, Silvina was still blindfolded, terrified, with her baby crying next to her. When they arrived, a doctor came and cut the umbilical cord. And she was made to walk up one or two flights of stairs before coming to the place where they would eventually remove the placenta. The guards insulted and threatened her as she was made to undress, made to clean up the mess she had made with her blood—the bed, the floor, her clothes, and to get rid of the placenta. The doctor who had "helped" her with her umbilical cord took off her blindfold, saying, "Now you're not missing anything," which Silvina took to mean that she would eventually be killed because she could identify her captors.

Silvina had arrived in the Pozo de Banfield, pozo meaning "hole" or "well," an appropriate name for a torture center into which people were tossed and never seen again. Silvina stayed with her baby that night in a separate section of the complex, and the next day she was put back into a cell, reunited once again with her friends of necessity, Julia and Elena. In each cell there were two to three women.

Although this was a very difficult time for Silvina, filled with stress and the possibility of immediate death, the time she spent in the Pozo was, relatively, a happier time for her and for the rest of the prisoners. She describes how she

> went visiting, because the doors were closed all day, but in the moment that they took you to the bathroom, we tricked the guards, and I was put with my baby in another cell, and we talked all afternoon long, all day long, with the two or three who were in each cell. When they took us out again to eat, for example, I stuck myself in a different cell. In this way I went visiting. We were there from May 5 or 6 until May 15. Then, they took everyone away.

If it is possible for a living being to be a symbol, then her child was a symbol for the woman prisoners. When all the habits and customs of everyday life had been outlawed, when their neighbors, families, husbands, had been stripped from them, and they were awaiting their own execution, the most basic and potent symbol of life, a baby, was somehow permitted. And for a short while they were a family, one child of many mothers, all placing their hopes and dreams on Silvina's liberation and survival.

It is impossible to know the thoughts that ran through Julia's mind as she held the child, impossible to track the feelings of her heart, her anguish, but she held the baby as the rest of the women did, held it close to her and loved it. Perhaps she thought of the children she had cared for in the girls' home in Córdoba, where they grew up in a much different institution; with so much against them, with physical and mental handicaps, they at least grew up with love and care, not surrounded by armed guards, ready to take them away at any moment. Perhaps it made her think of her own child she had been carrying for over five months, the hopes and dreams she had for it. What was the list of names she and Alberto had gone over and over, if it were a boy, if it were a girl?

She talked about the past, of happier times. As Julia held Silvina's baby, she described how she had looked on her wedding day, how she had felt, how her gown had looked so perfect. She talked about food as well, and they all took mental notes, exchanging recipes for when they would be back home with their families again, and they would cook for each other. They all gave Silvina their addresses and telephone numbers so that if she were indeed freed, she could tell their parents that they were all right, that they were still alive.

At times, Julia closed up from the rest of the women, and there seemed to be a great distance between them. Sometimes, Julia hardly seemed to be there. Silvina remembers:

> She had moments of depression, in which a lot of time went by without speaking. But that's not to say that she was badly off; rather, I think her character was like that. Remember, I didn't know her before. I think that her character was more introverted, quieter; she spoke less.

All in all, Silvina says that if there were one word to describe Julia—something Silvina seriously doubts—it would be "peace." It's difficult, she says, to take a person, complex and full of mystery, and give her one word to be known by. From late March, when Silvina arrived, until the night of May 15, 1977, when Julia was taken in a large transfer, never to be seen again, Julia was a dear friend, a mentor, a sister, always helping to make the days and the nights a bit more bearable, and Silvina will always remember her.

On May 18, Silvina was released along with her husband and small child. The man who freed them seemed to be nervous, as he said, "Don't believe everything you've seen and heard, because this was just to scare you a little."

VOICE 12

Eduardo Rabossi

*Former Subsecretary of Human Rights, Ministry of the
Interior, under President Raúl Alfonsín; former fellow at
the National Humanities Center, North Carolina.*

The issue of this sought-after justice is very difficult because I think
that the people, the majority of the people, would be more satisfied,
simply, by nothing more and nothing less, if the person who tortured
their son or daughter were identified, not those who invented the plan
and did all this. Let's call it satisfaction, a certain personal vengeance,
justifiable, to be able to say, "Yes, I know that whoever did this to my
son or my daughter or to my boyfriend or to my girlfriend, to my
father, or to whomever, is a prisoner or something bad is happening
to him."

The law of *Obediencia Debida*, for me as subsecretary, was the most bitter moment. I think that Alfonsín did what he did after a complete balancing of the pros and cons, et cetera, the reason that made Alfonsín for many people a fallen idol. In the end I always say that it's like in a game of American football or soccer. When the game is over, you could have kicked the ball here or there. Or a film. After seeing the film and knowing the whole story, afterward you can say, "Well, if you had just done this, you could have done it better."

It's possible. At best, it would have been preferable to have made a list of the ones who were very obviously responsible and end it there. After having dealt with relatives for nearly six years, I believe that the worst thing that can happen to someone is to make his son or daughter disappear. It's the worst, the impossibility of working out the grief, of being able to know what happened. You see, it's terrible. It's a type of punishment.

They didn't have sufficient evidence in order to pick out who was responsible, and the emphasis that Alfonsín always used was that politics was a way to give people confidence in the way justice works. CONADEP [the National Commission on the Disappearance of People] received a bit more than seven thousand denunciations, which can be added to an additional number in working with the international and national organizations of human rights, which reached to around nine thousand cases of disappeared. The obligation that CONADEP only partially fulfilled because of a lack of time (and that the Subsecretariat finally completed at the beginning of 1986) was to put all of these denunciations in the hands of the judiciary.

I would say in the first place that the person who disappears in these situations is the product of a strategy. The word *desaparecido* was invented in Guatemala and in Argentina, but we didn't invent the strategy, the immense strategy, in the massive way, you see, of Hitler. That is to say, what Hitler did was a similar strategy because the Jews were taken from their houses under the excuse that they were being taken to certain relocation areas. It's very similar to what happened here, these groups that presented themselves as police, as military, et cetera, a terrible chaos. The strategy consists in rounding up human beings.

Three friends of mine were unlucky enough that one night a group of people entered their house, and, well, they were taken away. And they said that they had been taken to such and such a division, that they were going to some police station, and I went there and there wasn't anyone there. This produces a psychological effect—that's what the strategy is trying to do—because you don't know what to do. The strategy is this, that the relatives, the families, the colleagues, don't know what to do. You don't know if you should make the whole affair public, or think not to and they'll release him in a few days, seven days, fifteen days. And if I make the affair public, it could be worse for him. The consequence of staying quiet could be that something happens to him. There's always a great period of indecision.

The *desaparecido* is an individual who has been the object of a strategy and has a counterpart in his friends, his relatives. A disappeared person is not the only *desaparecido*. It is the family member of the *desaparecido*. There is not a disappeared person without a counterpart in the family member, and these are the objectives of the disappearance. I would say that he is a ghost because a ghost has a lot to do with the unreal, no? The disappeared person has his own personal identity. Juan Pérez, Rodriguez, people from real cases. Real people, biographies, and faces. The photo albums of those human rights organizations are frightening. We made an album of the victims, but I still can't read it.

AUTHOR'S EPILOGUE

Who was Julia, then? Does this collection of anecdotes and visions come close to describing her? Or are these stories merely echoes sounding against the dark wall of memory, a few scattered glimpses, and then nothingness?

Was she the politically astute *militante* sharing a prison cell with Silvina, or the naive, young doctor who promised Luciano she would never charge her patients? Was she the dedicated altruist who bathed disabled children with Laura, or the desperate young wife who turned her back on her own brother because of the danger he posed for her and her husband? As with any personality, full of contradictions and complexities, Julia cannot be seen in her entirety. She was, perhaps, all of these things at once, as each person who knew Julia saw a different side to her, had different fears for her, held different hopes. Who she was is gone. Who she is now depends on who remembers her.

Why Julia was made to disappear is another lingering question. Did she fall in with the wrong crowd? Did she follow her brother, Luis Ignacio, a bit too far? Or was she just one more doctor working in a state-run hospital, someone who thought about the common good, and therefore was too dangerous for the military to let go by unchecked? Question after question remains unanswered, and yet that which might seem the most obvious—who killed Julia?—is not really a question at all.

In this world of shadows, we cannot know who pointed the gun at Julia's head, who put a bullet in her brain. But we do know who gave the orders, who directed the torture chambers, who buried the bodies. The commanders of the *desaparecedores*, the ones who made Julia and countless others disappear, were singled out at the trial of the Junta, and there can be no doubt as to their identity. There can also be no doubt that not one of those who murdered, electrocuted, raped, tossed people out of airplanes, sacked houses, or stole children during the Dirty War is in jail.

Well aware of his immunity, ex–de facto President Videla has recently been seen jogging in the park near the house where Julia's mother lives. Ex-General Camps, recently deceased—responsible for the deaths of an unknown number of adolescents in Buenos Aires—frequented the more chic restaurants of the city, fraternizing openly with the "in" crowd of Argentine society. And the leader of the death squad that terrorized Julia's home in Córdoba in 1975 was sighted a few weeks ago in a bar near where Julia's remains were finally buried. The word "justice" has a hollow sound to it when contemplating the disappeared.

But justice never was part of this investigation. Nor were vengeance, penalties, punishments. It has to do, more basically and more importantly, with memory and fear.

When I first met Julia's brother Manuel at his home in Buenos Aires, we sat in his small apartment, looking at old newspaper clippings, drinking tea, eating cookies, and talking about the past. As we sat chatting, Manuel excused himself for a moment and, saying that he might have something interesting for me, went into his bedroom. A few moments later, he came back carrying a cardboard box.

Several days after Julia had been kidnapped, the Montesinis went to the Clínica de Nuestra Señora de Luján to gather her belongings.

Everything was there, just as she had left it: reading glasses, agenda, books, notes. When Manuel returned home from the clinic, he packed it all away and stored it in his closet. He said that for years he couldn't look at what was inside, afraid of what he might find, afraid of what it would make him remember.

It was this box that Manuel brought to me that night, and together we opened it and began our search for Julia. He remembered. He cried. He was sorry for having opened the box, and he was overjoyed. Everything else followed from that night, that box. It was the catalyst for memory, and if it weren't for Manuel's desire to shout against the darkness of his sister's disappearance, her story would never have come about. As we sat on the living room floor, spreading out the notes, searching through the fragments, I remembered the boxes of skeletons in the cemetery morgue and wondered how many boxes such as Manuel's there were in Argentina. On how many shelves, in how many bedroom closets, lay fragments of other lives untouched, stories untold, because it's better left forgotten? How many Argentines still live with the family secret, still say *De eso, no se habla* ("This is not talked about") when their children ask, "Where is Uncle Juan?" or "Where is Aunt Luisa?" How many people live in pain and fear, still victims of the past?

That night, Manuel began to confront his pain, to break the unspoken taboos. He is still finding Julia, bits and pieces of her, as he continues talking to friends and acquaintances who knew his sister. His search for Julia will never end. If Julia's story, if Manuel's story, means anything at all, it is an invitation for the rest of those left behind to begin to open the boxes, to begin to talk. The guilty will not go to prison if this silence is broken. The murderers will not be put on trial again. But by asking these questions, memories will be released, and, so very important, lives of the dead will be remembered, while those of the living will be renewed. The answers hardly matter. But talk, talk, define the dark shadows that linger over every family, over every conscience that suffered during the Dirty War. Silence: there is too much silence in the unmarked graves in the cemetery of Avellaneda. . . .

INDEX

Latin American Studies/Human Rights

In 1977 "Julia" became one of the 30,000 victi[ms of] Argentina's most recent military dictatorship. Julia was a [young] physician and mother-to-be kidnapped from a medical clini[c and] found years later in a clandestine grave along with 334 [other] corpses. Who were those thousands of victims? Who was Julia?

By reconstructing Julia's life, Eric Stener Carlson gives voice [to] thousands of citizens who were "disappeared." In doing so, h[e] use the pseudonym "Julia" to protect the people she left be[hind.] Julia's poignant story is told through the emotional memor[ies of] childhood friends and family, classmates and colleagues, an ex-[lover] and fellow prisoners whose lives intersected with hers i[n the] government torture centers. Interspersed between the personal testimonies are the commentaries of a military general, a priest, a politician, a human rights activist, and a prosecuting attorney in the war crimes tribunal, giving her story a political and social context.

"I Remember Julia is a powerful and deeply moving portrayal of Argentina's dirty war, all the more unique and evocative for its focus on the life-and-death of one individual. It is impossible to read this and not come away with a sense of the profound human tragedy associated with this brutal period in Argentine history."

— Cynthia Arnson, senior program associate,
Latin American Program, The Woodrow
Wilson International Center for Scholars

Eric Stener Carlson is a Fellow for Physicians for Human Rights, working with the War Crimes Tribunal for the Former Yugoslavia in The Hague, The Netherlands. He previously spent two years in Buenos Aires, Argentina, one of them as a Fulbright Sc[holar,] conducting research and interviews for this book.

Cover design: Becky Baxendell
Printed in U.S.A.

Temple University Press
Philadelphia 19122
cloth ISBN 1-56639-430-9
paper ISBN 1-56639-437-6

ISBN 1-56639-437-6

90000

9 781566 394376